More Than
Little
Professors

More Than Little Professors

Children with Asperger Syndrome: In Their Own Words

Edited by
Lisa Barrett Mann, M.S. Ed.

Foreword by
Brenda Smith Myles, Ph.D.

Autism Asperger Publishing Company
P.O. Box 23173
Shawnee Mission, Kansas 66283-0173
www.asperger.net

©2008 Autism Asperger Publishing Company
P. O. Box 23173
Shawnee Mission, Kansas 66283-0173
www.asperger.net • 877-288-8254

Publisher's Cataloging-in-Publication

More than little professors : children with Asperger syndrome: in their own words / [edited by] Lisa Barrett Mann. -- 1st ed. -- Shawnee Mission, Kan. : Autism Asperger Pub. Co., c2008.
     p. ; cm.

     ISBN: 978-1-934575-25-3
     LCCN: 2008928392

     1. Asperger's syndrome in children. 2. Asperger's syndrome--Patients--Biography. I. Mann, Lisa Barrett.

RJ506.A9 M67   2008 2008928392
618.92/858832--dc22   0806

Cover art: © istockphoto; jammydesign

For David and Gary.

You are my superheroes.

"These children, and especially the intellectually gifted among them, undoubtedly have a special creative attitude towards language. They are able to express their own original experience in a linguistically original form. This is seen in the choice of unusual words which one would suppose to be totally outside the sphere of these children. It is also seen in newly formed or partially restructured expressions which can often be particularly accurate and perspicacious."

– Hans Asperger, 1944

Contents

Foreword

If you want to understand children with Asperger Syndrome, go directly to the source – the children themselves. They are our best teachers.

This book is a gift to anyone who seeks to understand this complex exceptionality that we have labeled Asperger Syndrome (AS). The words on the following pages offer the best information on AS that I have had the privilege to read. In addition, the children whose work appears here provide, in my estimation, a more accurate understanding of AS than many journal articles that I have read.

Some question whether those with AS have empathy. This book provides the answer – a definite yes. Do they care about others? Absolutely. Can the world sometimes be unkind in ways that children with AS should not have to endure? Tragically, yes. Do children and youth with AS have something special to offer the world? Undeniably, yes.

Why don't we know these things? Perhaps it is because we don't listen. It takes a special person to do so – someone who respects differences and, indeed, rejoices in them. Lisa Barrett

Mann is one of those people. A brilliant author in her own right, Lisa has chosen to let the words of those with AS teach us to understand and see that there are different perspectives.

Mindblindness, or an inability to take or understand others' perspectives, and lack of empathy are touted as hallmark characteristics of AS. Reading this book has taught me that neurotypical individuals are likely the ones who have mindblindness and lack empathy – we can't see the perspectives of children and youth with AS – that is, until now. Lisa's gift, *More Than Little Professors*, has the potential to remove our mindblindness and create empathy. The children you meet in this book can help us see the world in a way that may be more rich and perhaps, at times, more tragic. The words in this book provide wisdom.

Please read, enjoy, learn, laugh, and cry. Everything we need to know about AS is on these pages.

> **Brenda Smith Myles, Ph.D.,** a consultant with the Ziggurat Group, is the recipient of the 2004 Autism Society of America's Outstanding Professional Award and the 2006 Princeton Fellowship Award. She has written numerous articles and books on Asperger Syndrome and autism, including *Asperger Syndrome and Difficult Moments: Practical Solutions for Tantrums, Rage, and Meltdowns* (with Southwick) and *Asperger Syndrome and Adolescence: Practical Solutions for School Success* (with Adreon). The latter is the winner of the Autism Society of America's 2002 Outstanding Literary Work.

Preface

When I studied psychology in college in the early 1980s, we were taught that the incidence of autism was 1 in 10,000. People with autism, we were told, rarely spoke, and showed no emotion, nor any interest in other people. So it's little wonder that, after my son was born in 1995, I didn't associate his quirky behaviors with autism.

David said his first word ("more") at 4 months, knew all his letters by his first birthday, and by age 4 was talking about "inter-dimensional portals." I remember warning his first preschool teacher that he had "big emotions" – he could be the happiest kid on earth, or the saddest, or the angriest, but he was *never* unemotional. And he *loved* to talk to people. Or, more specifically, to talk *at* people. He desperately wanted to share his vast knowledge of Superman, and he told the stories with such feeling that the other preschoolers often listened in awe. But when it came time for recess, there was trouble. The other kids would try to play Superman with David, the teacher told us, but he'd quickly melt down, because they wouldn't stick to his script – and any deviation from the exact storyline of the comic book or cartoon was unacceptable to him.

By the time he was diagnosed with Asperger Syndrome in second grade, our brilliant little boy was spending much of his day staring into space, lost in complex fantasies about anime and video game characters. He could read way beyond his grade level, but he could barely write his name, and was quickly falling behind in other subjects – mostly because he often wasn't even aware of what was going on around him. I was shocked to learn that many other children exhibited similar eccentric behaviors, challenges, and talents – and that they were considered part of the "autism spectrum."

That was a scary time for our family, but we were lucky. We had resources that many families don't – nearby specialists, good health insurance, and lots of support at school. My son spent third grade in a self-contained classroom with five other children with Asperger Syndrome, and a teacher who really "got" them. The change was remarkable. David learned to write. He started making honor roll. And our little boy, who had become increasingly depressed and anxious, was suddenly a happy child with friends and playdates. By fourth grade, he and his classmates were going to general education classes for math and social studies, and by fifth grade, for most of the day. But the friendships remained. These children had developed a tight bond. And, meanwhile, so had their moms.

Typically, when a child exhibits problem behaviors, the first one to get blamed is Mom. Teachers, family members, and even strangers just assume that your child has anxiety attacks or meltdowns because you're overprotective or don't discipline him. That's especially true for kids with Asperger Syndrome. People think that, because our kids have such mature speech, they should have the mature behavior to match. Even after you have a diagnosis, there are always people who refuse to believe that there's a neurological reason behind your child's behavior.

So when the mothers of children with Asperger Syndrome get together, there's often a special connection. They don't judge you when you can't get your 11-year-old to swallow a pill, or when your 5-year-old has a huge meltdown at the bookstore because you refused to buy him the $175 unabridged dictionary. They cheer when you tell them that, for the very first time, your high school student remembered to turn in his homework without extra reminders from the teacher. And they share their own stories about things their children said and did. Those stories can be hysterically funny or heartbreaking, but they're always fascinating. Because – through their words and actions – these kids are telling you how their minds work.

Today, there are many books and articles in which experts hold forth on what Asperger Syndrome is and how it "presents" in children. But while children with Asperger Syndrome all have some traits in common (e.g., difficulties with social skills and nonverbal communication), they also vary tremendously, just like all kids do. If you've seen one child with Asperger Syndrome ... you've seen one child with Asperger Syndrome. Perhaps that's part of the reason why many children with Asperger's still aren't being diagnosed until they are 11 or even older (often not until high school or adulthood). And that's unacceptable – because the earlier these kids get appropriate intervention, the better their chances of growing up to be happy, successful adults.

This book shares the words, writings, and artwork of more than 60 children – toddlers through teens – with Asperger Syndrome. It started out with quotes and poems from my son and his classmates. Then I put out the word through a few Asperger support groups and online discussion boards that I was looking for material, and submissions started pouring in from across the country, and even Canada and Australia. But it wasn't just parents contributing stories. Many children wrote to me too, excited about an opportunity to share their thoughts and feelings.

Today, at least 1 in 150 school children are diagnosed with an autism spectrum disorder – many of them, with Asperger Syndrome. These are smart, loving children with huge potential, whose brains just happen to be wired a little differently from their typically developing peers'. Through their quotes, their stories, and their poetry, they're giving you a unique opportunity in this book to "get inside their heads" and experience the world as they do. It's my hope that, with that experience, you will also gain a new understanding and appreciation of these awesome kids.

– Lisa Barrett Mann

Introduction

All the quotes, stories, poems, and essays in this book come from children and teens diagnosed with Asperger Syndrome or high-functioning autism. Although the cover lists me as "editor," in most cases, children's writing appears in this book *exactly* as they submitted it. The only editing I have done is to occasionally break long submissions into paragraphs, add some commas here and there, and correct the odd typo. The wording is completely the children's. That's because the purpose of this book is to give the reader insight into how these children's minds work – not into how an editor *thinks* they should work. (It should be noted, however, that, because some of the poems and stories were written as school assignments, they may have been "corrected" by teachers before they were submitted.)

At the beginning of each chapter is a quotation from a famous individual who is reputed to have exhibited at least some of the characteristics of Asperger Syndrome. I include their quotes to illustrate how our society today has been positively impacted by people who "think differently."

Asperger Syndrome

Until 1994, when Asperger's Disorder (often referred to as Asperger Syndrome) was added to the American Psychiatric Association's *Diagnostic and Statistical Manual of Mental Disorders* (DSM), only a few academics were aware of this fascinating condition. Today, many people are aware of Asperger's, thanks to the increased media coverage – and increased prevalence – of all autism spectrum disorders. But, sadly, awareness doesn't always equal understanding. It's not uncommon to hear someone say Asperger Syndrome is "like Rain Man" (the character portrayed by Dustin Hoffman in the 1988 movie of the same name had autism and savant skills, not Asperger Syndrome). Others dismiss the diagnosis completely, thinking it's just a trendy label given to gifted, nerdy kids.

Well, any parent or teacher of a child with Asperger Syndrome can tell you that this condition is very real. But it's not a "one size fits all" kind of diagnosis. Every child with Asperger's is unique. These children share some characteristics, and some challenges, but they vary tremendously too – in their abilities, their likes and dislikes, their challenges, and their personalities.

How Is Asperger Syndrome Diagnosed?

There's no medical test for Asperger Syndrome. You can't tell a person has it by looking at blood work or an MRI. A diagnosis is generally based on the child (or adult) meeting a standard set of criteria. In the United States, the most widely used criteria today are from the DSM-IV-TR (4th edition; text revision; American Psychiatric Association, 2000), which specifies that

DSM-IV-TR Diagnostic Criteria for 299.80 Asperger's Disorder

A. Qualitative impairment in social interaction, as manifested by at least two of the following:
    (1) marked impairment in the use of multiple nonverbal behaviors such as eye-to-eye gaze, facial expression, body postures, and gestures to regulate social interaction
    (2) failure to develop peer relationships appropriate to developmental level
    (3) a lack of spontaneous seeking to share enjoyment, interests, or achievement with other people (e.g., by lack of showing, bringing, or pointing out of objects of interest to other people)
    (4) lack of social or emotional reciprocity

B. Restricted repetitive and stereotyped patterns of behavior, interests, and activities as manifested by at least one of the following:
    (1) encompassing preoccupation with one or more stereotyped and restricted patterns of interest that is abnormal either in intensity or focus
    (2) apparently inflexible adherence to specific, nonfunctional routines or rituals
    (3) stereotyped and repetitive motor mannerisms (e.g., hand or finger flapping or twisting, or complex whole-body movements)
    (4) persistent preoccupation with parts or objects

C. The disturbance causes clinically significant impairment in social, occupational, or other important areas of functioning.

D. There is no clinically significant general delay in language (e.g., single words used by age 2 years, communicative phrases used by age 3 years).

E. There is no clinically significant delay in cognitive development or in the development in age-appropriate self-help skills, adaptive behavior (other than in social interaction), and curiosity about the environment in childhood.

F. Criteria are not met for another specific Pervasive Developmental Disorder or Schizophrenia.

Source: American Psychiatric Association. (2000). *Diagnostic and statistical manual of mental disorders (4th ed. – text revision)*. Washington, DC: Author.

the child must have two or more symptoms of "impairment in social interaction," and one or more symptoms of narrow, repetitive behaviors or interests (see box, p. 7). Basically, it's the same diagnostic criteria as those used for classical autism, except that to be diagnosed with autism, the child must also have delayed speech or other communication difficulties, and have experienced difficulties in social interaction, social use of language, or play behaviors before age 3. Moreover, while a child with autism may also be diagnosed with mental retardation, under DSM-IV-TR, a child with Asperger's may not.

But as research into Asperger Syndrome continues to evolve, many experts today say that some children with Asperger's *do* experience early speech delays. Certainly, their speech tends to be qualitatively different from that of other children the same age, and they have great difficulty carrying on back-and-forth conversations, especially with peers. Although most have normal IQs, and a sizeable number have IQs in the gifted range, a small percentage of individuals with Asperger Syndrome have mild mental retardation.

Confused yet? You're not alone. Perhaps that's why one common (albeit oversimplified) approach to diagnosing children with impaired social skills and repetitive behaviors has become: "Had cognitive or language delays? Diagnose autism. Has normal IQ and was talking at a normal age? Diagnose Asperger's." The truth is that the jury is still out over the question of whether Asperger Syndrome and high-functioning autism are two distinct disorders, and if so, how they should be accurately identified. There is also some speculation that we might be looking at *multiple* disorders – not just two – with similar symptoms.

In a sense, though, the debate is largely academic. The fact is, Asperger Syndrome often is *not* difficult to recognize; it's just hard to quantify. There are plenty of cases where the symptoms are subtle, or a child has additional issues that may blur the diagnosis. But experts who have spent a lot of time with children with Asperger Syndrome (clinicians, teachers, even parents) are often able to pick up on signs of the disorder within minutes of meeting the child for the first time. While it would obviously be irresponsible for anyone to make a clinical diagnosis without a thorough evaluation, there's no denying that, an awful lot of the time, "we know it when we see it."

So What Does Asperger Syndrome Really Look Like?

As mentioned earlier, no two children with Asperger Syndrome are exactly alike. But certain characteristics are considered "prototypical, " including the following.

- **One or more all-consuming special interests**. Yes, lots of little girls love horses and lots of little boys love Spider-Man. But a child with Asperger Syndrome will pursue his special interest with an intensity far beyond that of a "neurotypical" child (i.e., a child without an autism spectrum disorder or other neurological difference). Children with Asperger's often pursue their interests with more determination than a new lawyer studying for the bar exam. Often their emphasis is on gathering as many facts about a given subject as possible. And, while the ability doesn't always carry over to, say, the multiplication tables, their ability to memorize facts about their special interest can be staggering.

Whether it's an interest that's common to other children their age, such as video games, or something more idiosyncratic, such as dentistry or deep fat fryers, the obsessive interests of children with AS typically bring them much comfort and happiness. The downside is that these interests can interfere with their ability to function in the "real world," where kids are expected to be able to converse on a wide range of subjects and to study whatever the teacher tells them to study.

While a child's special interest can be in any area, a handful of areas come up quite frequently, including animals or dinosaurs, branches of science and technology, technical data on specific mechanical devices (e.g., vacuum cleaners), modes of transportation (cars, trains, etc.), train schedules, video/computer games, movies (especially science fiction), Japanese animation, TV shows, and superheroes.

- **Superficially perfect speech.** Children with Asperger Syndrome often have very advanced vocabularies for their age. They may use adult phrasing or very formal speech patterns that they've picked up from books or movies, which can be awkward or inappropriate when they're trying to interact with their peers. Some children with Asperger's tend to talk in a very dry, monotone manner. Others tend to over-emote, using somewhat exaggerated words and tone of voice for normal conversation. Still others have surprisingly immature voices for their age.

- **A tendency to lecture and difficulty carrying on back-and-forth conversations.** Now you can see why children with Asperger's are often referred to as "little professors." Take a kiddo with an encyclopedic knowledge of a very specific, perhaps arcane subject, who likes to lecture to you about it, using very advanced, adult-like vocabulary. Sounds like a real prodigy, right? In some ways, yes. But that same kiddo might not be able to carry on a simple back-and-forth conversation with a schoolmate about recess, classmates, or his summer vacation.

- **A desire for friends, but difficulty making friends.** Children with classic autism often seem uninterested in, or even unaware of, others. Children with Asperger Syndrome, however, typically want to have friends, but their social awkwardness gets in the way. Let's face it, the 7-year-old who runs up to a bunch of his classmates on the playground and announces that "The Dyson DC14 upright with Root Cyclone™ technology has 12 amps and a bin capacity of 0.71 gallons" will have a difficult time making a social connection. But it is hard for him to understand why. After all, that bit of vacuum cleaner knowledge brings him great pleasure, so why wouldn't the other kids want to hear about it, too?

- **Difficulty interpreting social cues.** Communication involves a lot more than words. People communicate as much – sometimes more – information through their hand gestures, facial expressions, body language, and tone of voice, as they do through their words. Neurotypical children learn much of this instinctively; for example, no one has to tell Joey that when his teacher gives him the "evil eye," she wants him to stop talking to his neighbor and get back to work. But many children with Asperger Syndrome don't have the same innate understanding of nonverbal communication. Depending on her degree of difficulty in this area, the child with AS may be able to read major emotions (anger, sadness) in another's face, but miss subtleties such as when a person slowly backs away, it is an indication that he wants to end a conversation. Another child with Asperger's may be oblivious to even basic facial expressions such as a furrowed brow meaning a person is angry or disapproving. Occasionally, a child with Asperger Syndrome uses inappropriate nonverbal cues himself, such as laughing and smiling when he feels nervous, rather than happy.

- **Overly literal interpretation of language.** Factual information tends to be the forté of children with Asperger's. But reading between the lines – understanding what the author implies, but doesn't come right out and say – can be an area of difficulty. Kids with Asperger Syndrome tend to be very literal thinkers – they say what they think and expect others to do the same. Similes and metaphors can pose a particular challenge. As a result, many have to be specifically taught that "Don't spill the beans" is not actually a warning against dropping legumes.

- **Adherence to specific routines and need for predictability.** Most of us have certain routines that we're almost unaware of. For example, you may always put on your right sock first, then your left, then your right shoe, and finally your left shoe. If you were suddenly asked to do "left sock, left shoe, right sock, right shoe," you could probably do it without too much difficulty, even if it felt a little strange. Children with Asperger's, on the other hand, often have routines that they "need" to complete in order to feel okay. One child might get upset if Mom takes a different route home from the daycare center than usual. Another might have a meltdown if asked to drink his milk out of a red sippy cup instead of a blue one. A middle schooler who normally is very well mannered might "lose it" on days when the class schedule is changed to accommodate standardized testing.

- **Need for "completeness."** A child with Asperger Syndrome also may find it stressful or upsetting to stop in the middle of something – whether it's turning off a video that he's seen a million times before or putting away an unfinished worksheet when the bell rings. For some, the distress of being forced to "move on" without completing an activity can linger for hours. For others, it can be a sure-fire route to a full-scale meltdown.

- **Sensory difficulties.** Individuals with Asperger Syndrome often experience sensory input differently than neuro-typical individuals. Professionals refer to this as "sensory processing" or "sensory integration" difficulties. Many children with Asperger's are overly sensitive to bright light, loud noises, certain smells and tastes, and even textures. (Sock seams and clothing labels can make some kids so uncomfortable that they seem unable to think about anything other than getting the offending garments off.) Haircuts can be terrifying and downright painful for these children (and traumatic for everyone in the barber shop). Other children with AS are *under*sensitive to stimuli, and may seek out intense activities that will "register" with their nervous system, such as spinning in circles, bumping into walls (or other kids!), climbing, or running. And to make it even more confusing, some kids are oversensitive to some stimuli and undersensitive to others. Or they may be fine with a sensation one day, and cry out in pain from it the next. They're not being difficult – their nervous systems are.

- **Motor clumsiness.** Many children with Asperger Syndrome are physically awkward and clumsy. Physical education and recess – the times many students look forward to all day – can be torture for the kids with Aspeger's. Fine-motor skills, particularly handwriting, can also be problematic. These difficulties are frequently seen as an extension of sensory processing problems. For example, it's hard to kick a ball if you can't sense exactly where your foot is in relation to your body. And it's hard to write an essay if holding the pencil is painful, or if you have trouble feeling the pencil between your fingers.

The Upside of Asperger Syndrome

Because Asperger Syndrome is considered a "disorder," experts tend to define it by its difficulties and deficits. But let's look at it from a different point of view: the positives, or the "upside." Individuals with Asperger Syndrome tend to have:

- **An encyclopedic knowledge of their area of expertise.** Today, society pushes for everyone to be "well rounded."

But is that really what we want? If someone's going to fix your computer, sequence your DNA, or translate a contract you're about to sign with a foreign company, what's more important – her thorough, exacting knowledge of her craft or her "well-roundedness"?

- **Single-minded focus and determination.** If there's one thing a kid with Asperger Syndrome tends to have, it's stick-to-it-iveness. While so many people flit from one activity to another, individuals with Asperger's appreciate the importance of finishing what they start.

- **A straightforward approach to communication.** You know where you stand with a person with Asperger Syndrome. He says what he means! That can be pretty refreshing, especially today, when everyone from Fortune 500 CEOs to high-ranking government officials seem to specialize in obfuscation.

- **A fierce dedication to their friends and loved ones.** People with AS may have difficulty making social connections, but once they do connect, they are often very loyal and devoted friends and spouses. While some neurotypical individuals seem to prefer the earliest stages of relationships – the "chase" and the novelty of a getting to know a new person – those with AS tend to be more interested in enduring qualities and comfortable bonds.

- **A nonconformist – and often quite creative – point of view and a quirky sense of humor.** Individuals with Asperger Syndrome don't just think outside the box. They may fail to see the box, or dismiss it as pointless.

Such an approach to life can open up a whole new world of possibilities that the rest of us may have missed because we have trouble seeing anything BUT the box.

Of course, everything written above is a generalization. No two individuals with Asperger Syndrome are the same. The kids who contributed to this book could grow up to be computer scientists, film makers, government workers, grocery store clerks, musicians, even comedians. But they're all unique, fascinating, lovable kids. So much more than just "little professors."

By Allura

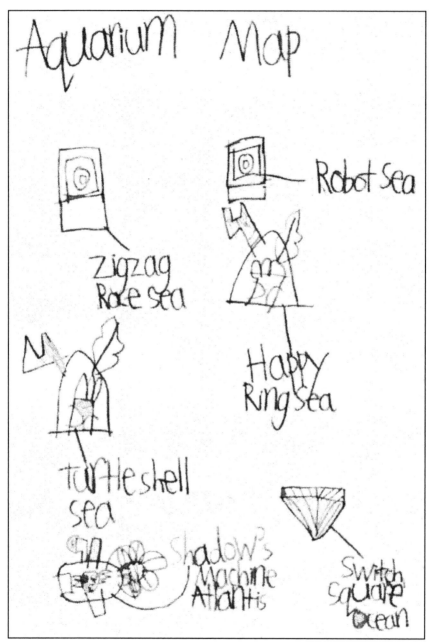

By Colin

A Way With Words

"*I always thought I'd like my own tombstone to be blank. No epitaph, and no name. Well, actually, I'd like it to say 'figment.'*"

– *Andy Warhol*

One of the reasons why children with Asperger Syndrome are often referred to as "little professors" is that they tend to have very advanced vocabularies and formal speech patterns. Many of our children are charmed and fascinated by the world of words and take great care to use terms precisely. Sometimes, "precisely" means recreating the exact tone, inflection, and even *accent* that was used when they first heard a phrase! (That's why, when my 5-year-old got frustrated, it sometimes sounded like he was channeling Yosemite Sam: "Dagnabbit!")

When our kids are little, this precocious speech can be pretty adorable. But as they get older, it can become a source of teasing. So, while we never want to discourage our children from expanding their vocabularies, we also want to teach them that we alter our speech (tone, volume, vocabulary, and content), depending on where we are and whom we're with.

While most children have to learn the difference between an "inside" and an "outside" voice, a child with Asperger's might have to memorize a plethora of other rules about what's appropriate in different settings – rules that other children usually pick up without being directly taught. And sometimes we parents and teachers have to modify our reactions to their words, so we help them, rather than hinder them. This might mean that when your 14-year-old uses the "s" word, you don't tell him "Don't ever say that again!," but instead counsel him that it's okay to use cuss words when he's just with his buddies, but that it's not okay when grownups are present. (Because, let's face it, most 14-year-old boys DO cuss around each other, and the child with Asperger's has enough challenges without being mocked for saying "Oh sugar!" when he's mad!)

What a Dumb Question!

When Daniel* was 4, two of his Montessori aides were pregnant. One day, Daniel was walking around sticking his tummy way out.

Teacher: "Daniel, do you have a baby in your tummy?"

Daniel: "No, silly, I don't have a uterus!"

(No one knew where Daniel had picked up this anatomically correct terminology!)

* Daniel is now in college, with a large scholarship.

Another Dumb Question (Boy, we adults are annoying!)

Breanna, age 3, was taking a LONG time in the bathroom.

Dad (who was busting to go), called out, "Bree, are you doing a wee or a poo?"

"I am defecating !" she replied.

Computer Language

Duncan, age 11, often tells his grandmother exactly what he means:

When he doesn't want to talk to anyone:

"I'm offline."

When he's hurt:

"Look, I'm damaged."

When he's annoyed with his grandmother:

"Nana, my happiness is at 0 percent!"

Where Forrest Comes From

Mom can't even remember the incident that prompted her to correct Forrest's manners. But she clearly remembers his response — one of his early attempts at sarcasm:

Forrest: "Where I come from, RUDE is polite."
(age 4)

Letting 'Em Down Easy

At age 4, Breanna's parents had a hard time getting her to eat vegetables. One day, they were pleasantly surprised to see that she had actually tried her broccoli. But then she put her fork down and announced:

"Mum, Dad. I am afraid that this broccoli is just not for me."

❖   ❖   ❖

Letting 'Em Down Easy, Part 2

When David was 4, he tried to explain to his parents why he wasn't interested in learning to ride his bike:

"Mom, Dad, I'm sorry, but riding's just not my style."

That's a Lot of Love!

David and Forrest don't know each other, but it sounds like they were both fans of the book Guess How Much I Love You *by Sam McBratney.*

David: "Guess how much I love you, Mom? I love you
(age 4)   right up to the moon!"

Mom: "I love *you* right up to the moon and back!"

David: "I love *you* all the way to Florida and swimming
           in Aunt Gail's pool!"

(Mom was then stumped. In David's view, NOTHING could beat going to Florida and swimming in Aunt Gail's pool!)

Forrest: "I love you all the way to the moon and back
(age 3)   googolplex* times!"

---

*Googolplex is a real number. *Googol* is 10 to the hundredth power, or 1 followed by 100 zeroes. *Googolplex* is 10 to the googol power. Coincidentally, *googolplex* was also one of David's favorite words when he was little.

A Yummy Number

Kaede, at age 4

"Mama?! I looooove pie! It's my favorite number!"

By Andrew

Quotes from Forrest

Forrest's mom had the foresight to write down many of the cute or impressive remarks he made as a preschooler and was kind enough to share them with us.

"I sometimes have short-term memory loss, and I sometimes remember things for a long time."

– Forrest, at age 4

"Mommy, I want a Cheerio ... my tummy already digested for a long time."

– Forrest, at age 3

Mom was making a batch of cinnamon scones with Forrest. He leaned over the mixing bowl to smell the dough and remarked:

"It's the sweet smell of success, right?!"

– Forrest, at age 3

It was holiday season, and Forrest was having a hard time getting to sleep. Finally, Mom went upstairs to his bedroom and asked him why he was still awake:

"The Christmas lights illuminate the ceiling over the windows."

– Forrest, at age 4

Forrest coloring a picture of an Easter Bunny (and, indeed, coloring the IRIS portion of the bunny's eye):

"Mom, I'm coloring the IRIS pink."

– Forrest, at age 4

"Is metal an ENGINEER of electricity?"

then, quickly correcting himself ...

"Is metal a CONDUCTOR of electricity?"

– Forrest, at age 4

Division of Labor

Rob, at age 16

Rob and his stepfather were arguing over who had done the most housework.

Step Dad: "I loaded the dishwasher!"

Rob: "Well, I'm the one who activated it!"

Sisters Are for Teasing

Will, at age 10

Will's big sister had decided to shave her legs for the first time. Half way through the process, she got distracted and decided to finish the second leg later. That led 10-year-old Will to come up with nicknames for her legs: "Hairy" and "Barey."

Wiring Problems

Dylan, at age 5

When Dylan was 5 years old, his doctor didn't recognize his differences as Asperger Syndrome, but did understand that he was "wired differently." He tried to explain to Dylan that he had "more wires than most people" in his brain.

Dylan replied: "Too many wires isn't my problem. It's not enough insulation!"

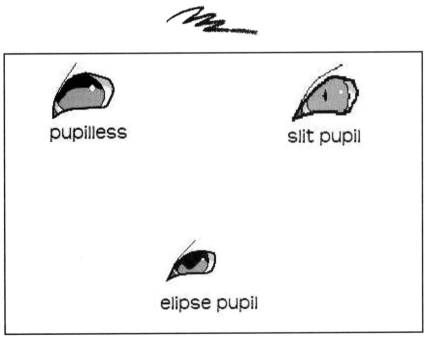

By Andrew

Moon Cheese

David, at age 2

Every day, with lunch and dinner, 2-year-old David would taste his slices of American cheese and say (with a British accent):

"Wensleydale? No, no, no."

Then, frowning he'd take another bite.

"Stilton? No, no, no."

After his third bite, he'd look baffled and mumble:

"It's like no cheese I've ever tasted!"

Finally, after a few more bites, he'd declare:

"I know, it's moon cheese!" and happily eat the rest.

Some folks might have been baffled by David's discerning palate. But Mom and Dad knew that David was reenacting a scene from Wallace and Gromit, A Grand Day Out, *one of the many videos he knew by heart.*

Mind Reading

Forrest, at age 5

Mom: "Did your kindergarten teacher like your
          Show & Tell today?

Forrest: "I don't know ... I'm not a mind reader."

When Forrest said this, he hadn't yet been diagnosed with Asperger Syndrome, and Mom had never even heard of it. Today, his mom finds the quote ironic, given that people with Asperger's are thought to have poor "theory of mind" – trouble knowing what others are thinking.

Wave Hello to the Ocean

Maxim, at age 4

Upon reaching the beach,

Maxim: "Look, Mom! The ocean is waving!"

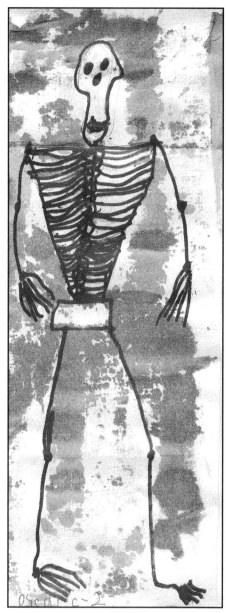

By "SuperRock"

Sensory
Experiences

"My sore throats are always worse than anyone's."
– Jane Austen

Although it's not considered a "symptom" of Asperger Syndrome or autism, "sensory integration dysfunction" (or "sensory processing disorder") is a common challenge for children on the spectrum. They may be either over-responsive or under-responsive to sensory stimuli such as light, temperature, noise, smells, tastes, and textures.

These sensory difficulties are neurologically based. Normally, when we take in information through our senses (sight, hearing, etc.), our brains organize and interpret the information and then signal our body to respond appropriately. For example, if you accidentally touch a hot iron, your nervous system will automatically signal your hand to pull away.

For children with sensory processing difficulties, however, the nervous system misinterprets the sensory input, and in turn triggers an inappropriate response. If a child's nervous system is over-responsive to a certain sensation, it can trigger a "fight or flight" response, resulting in a meltdown or panic. If her system in under-responsive, she may seem impervious to pain, or she may seek out extreme sensory experiences. Surprisingly, the same child can be over-responsive to some stimuli and under-responsive to others.

While a child can have any number or combination of sensory processing problems, parents of children on the spectrum often report that their children:

- crave heavy pressure such as bear hugs, but dislike being touched lightly
- want to spin or swing excessively
- are overly sensitive to sunlight
- panic at the sound of a fire alarm (even when they're warned it's coming)
- will only eat a very limited number of foods (perhaps only foods of a certain color or texture)
- can't tolerate sock seams, clothing labels, or clothes that are even slightly stiff or scratchy
- hear (and are disturbed by) sounds other people barely notice, such as the hum of fluorescent lights
- quickly become overwhelmed in crowded places, such as shopping malls or school cafeterias

Summer

By David, at age 9

Summer is nature's hot torture
to people who hate heat.

Foods

By Evelyn, at age 8

Ice Cream
yummy, licking, eating
sundae, treat, vegetable, health
smelling, squishing, steaming
yucky, bitter
Asparagus

Thick Walls

By Will, at age 9

Thick walls
Give peace and quiet
To sore ears
When noisy kids yell as loud as a 1700's machine

Gum

By Lars, at age 5

Gum is like a chew toy for people.

Excerpt From Elizabeth's e-Journal

(at age 16)

4-6-06

just getting to the 300 hallway after I left class when the FIRE ALARM went off. I sprinted outside, listening to jeers of "yeah, run! the school's really on fire this time!" "Oh yeah, there's *really* a fire!" ... as if I didn't know.
so that basically SUCKED. eventually pulled myself together enough to go to my 6th hr – English. which I love the class. even if the language isn't my favorite. sensory overload. so I did what I could. mainly tried to focus on only SOUND as we listened to a tape of a short story. didn't know.

headed to choir afterwards to ask one quick question ... don't even remember what it was anymore. and the fire alarm went off again. I was right in the choir room or right outside. I did a lot worse with that one. ran outside. I'm really searching to find out what I'm supposed to get out of these things. I guess it's just a reminder that my friends are there for me. admitted, that was a bit much. and then it went off again. it was Horrible. If you are the one pulling it, just please stop it.

aside from my ears on fire, things are all right now. three-day-weekend. I hung around school until Emily finished diving at 5. but due to those fire drills, I missed the AP Euro review session. and I didn't get anyone to tape it. dangit. those are important. these fire drills interfere with my learning. it's not just a prank anymore. or a technical problem, as the admins claim. ya know, if it's a tekkie thing, why does it only go off during school? you'd think it'd go off at night and then we'd hear about it when we came back ...

Plop Plop

By Max, at age 8

Plop ... Plop ... Slap ... Slap ...
The sounds I hear as my body
Cuts through the water after my dive
The sound of the ocean rings in my ears
I tilt my head to let the water exit
Fizz ... fizz ...trickle ... trickle ...
Plop ... plop ... plop ...
Screaming, splashing, laughing
The sounds that are music to my ears
When I play at the pool.

Body Noises

By Will, at age 9

A red cell leaves the heart ...
ba-beat ... ba-beat ...
And starts a journey of incredible sounds ...
ba-beat ... ba-beat ...
1st stop, the brain
zap ... zap ... the sound of thinking
2nd stop, the throat
gulp ... gulp ... as food passes through
3rd stop, the stomach
gurgle ... gurgle ... as digestion begins
4th stop, the intestines
slurp ... slurp ... nutrients are absorbed
5th stop, the interior of the bones
clink ... clink ... allows for movement
6th stop, the lungs
suck in ... suck out ... inhale, exhale
A red cell returns to the heart
ba-beat ... ba-beat
As the journey comes to a pause
ba-beat ... ba-beat ...
My personal, favorite sound.

The Woods

By Adam G, at age 9

The woods, dark and scary
and the path is slippery and hard

The woods, like I am in a box
with no holes

and I hear something behind me ...
but it was only a leaf crashing to the ground.

The Woods.

The Sound of the Rain

By Claire, at age 17

The sound of the rain has gone awry.
When I stand in it, I am dry.

By Zak

Many children on the spectrum find that swinging soothes them or allows them to organize their thoughts. But Andrew's reaction reminds us that you should never assume that every child with autism or Asperger Syndrome will have the same reaction.

Swing Time

Andrew K, at age 2

Andrew was 2 when his baby brother was born. One spring day, Mom was putting Matt into the baby swing outside when Andrew, red-faced and nearly in tears, ran up, grabbed the swing, and with eloquence previously unheard from his lips, shouted: "Don't hurt my baby brother! I love him!"

Mom says that's the first clue she had that something was "wrong" with Andrew's dislike of the baby swing when he was an infant.

"The Usual"

David, at age 9

David had insisted on the same meal ("The Usual") for nearly every breakfast, lunch, and dinner for the past six years:

- Peanut butter (creamy) and jelly (grape) on (soft) whole-wheat bread
- 2 slices of Kraft (yellow) Deluxe American Cheese, *not* individually wrapped (Each slice had to be perfect, with no corners broken off and no wrinkles or tears.)
- Fruit (He was flexible here – it could be seedless grapes, a banana, canned peaches, or raisins. But only on days when he was feeling especially adventurous could it be a sliced apple.)
- A glass of skim milk or orange juice (no pulp!)

However, at a fast food restaurant, he would only eat:
- Chicken nuggets
- French fries
- Milk (or apple juice, in a pinch)

And at sit-down restaurant, David would only eat:
- A yellow American cheese sandwich on white bread ("not grilled, not toasted, just a plain grilled cheese sandwich – not grilled")
- French fries
- Milk

And remember how Mom always said, "When he gets hungry enough, he'll eat it"? Not this kid. He would starve rather than eat peanut butter and jelly or chicken nuggets in a sit-down restaurant. Know why?

David: "Because that's what I do!"

Today, at age 12, David has expanded his diet to include pizza, mozzarella sticks, and chicken in non-nugget form!

Seeing Is Believing

By Connor, at age 9

"I see the sound of love."

(while hugging his mother)

Darkness

By Zak, at age 9

I'm wicked, cruel, and I hide in the
Barren shadows. I am a ruthless, vile villain.
I bring fear, and death.
NOBODY CAN STAND MY WRATH OF CHAOS

Sunlight

By Zak, at age 9

I shimmer in the sky. I
Have a joyful, warm
Heart. Because I'm so
Jovial, the Earth is happy too.

The Stream

By Zak, at age 10

The stream.
The cool spiritual water claims your soul ... the birds sing
melodies
In the shining Sun ... the smell of the pine trees thriving
helps
Appreciate nature

No Wonder He Didn't Want It!

Mom: "Do you want cheese?"

Forrest: "Is it American?"
(age 4)

Mom: "Yes."

Forrest: "No. Last time it tasted like Silly Putty."

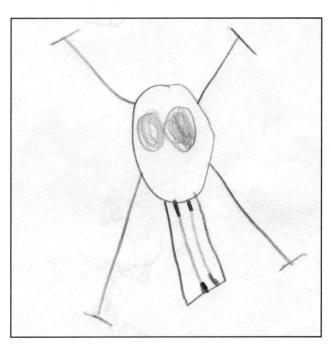

By Adam M

By Allura

Poetry

"Nor do I hear in my imagination the parts successively, I hear them all at once. What a delight this is! All this inventing, this producing, takes place in a pleasing, lively dream."
— *Wolfgang Amadeus Mozart*

"**E**xperts" often say that children with Asperger Syndrome are not creative. Perhaps they say that because kiddos with Asperger's so love repetition, whether it's reciting dialogue from a video or reading the same book over and over again. But the love of repetition and the ability to create something new and artistic don't have to be mutually exclusive. Some children express their creativity quite freely, through words, art, or music. Others are less effusive, but we should never just assume that it is because they do not have the ability. Of course, not everyone's an artist. But some have amazing talents that they just haven't tapped into yet.

While there are many poems scattered throughout this book, I've gathered several together in this chapter to illustrate the range and creativity that can be found among children on the spectrum.

By Zak

Animals

By Khalid, at age 7

A thunder of wolves clap at my window.
A tornado of foxes is spinning towards me.
A tsunami of sharks crashes onto the coastal beach.
A sleet of deer pass by me.
A lightning bolt of cheetahs flash by.
Raindrops of worms pelt down on my face.
A hail of snow leopards play tag with me.
A blizzard of leopards race with me.
A fog of frogs play leapfrog with me.

A Halloween Poem

By Avery, at age 8

A little bat sat on a ghost eating his girls and wae.
A pumpkin was on candy-cane licking it up.

Desert

By Zak, at age 9

I shine over this vacant waste land.
Death is written in the red and gold sand.
Scorpions rule this grave yard.
Nobody who had come here survived the experience.

Universe

By Zak, at age 9

An unknown universe, created
The universe as nobody has ever seen
It before
Strange matter lives across
Its endless corners. A space so
Lost in time. The galaxy trembles
With dark fear.

Shadows

By Kirby, at age 9

Shadows are black clones
that follow people when the
light falls just right.

Star

By Robyn, at age 9

A star is a white dish
a shooting, sparkling wish
a sight to behold
a story to be told.

Space

By Will, at age 9

Space is as black as shut eyes.
The mysteries are left to the
imagination.

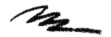

Metaphor Poem

By Patrick, at age 8

A volcano is a funnel
turned upside down
spitting lava to the ground.

Rain

By Zak, at age 9

I hide behind the white
clouds. The raindrops seem
like diamonds, falling from
the periwinkle colored sky.
When the rain ceases to
Fall I watch the rainbow
Climb its way down

Lightening

By Zak, at age 9

At the canyon, people and animals gaze at me in
Horror. As lightning, I watch as fire BLAZES when
I strike. Wolves howl. A gust of wind
Rages, and everyone trembles as
A thunder clap echos. I'm
              Unstoppable

This poem describes how a medication affected Abigail's memory.
(After reading this, her doctor had her discontinue the medication.)

Lamenting Lost Thoughts

By Abigail, at age 12

I don't know where I am in my thoughts.
They lead me on, grasping at a fragile whisper,
A whisper of a thought I thought I knew
But really, I don't see the whisper anymore,
I am stranded in a new land, one of thoughts of old,
Mixed together to form a mass of stewing ideas, memories,
Things I half remember, things I used to think,
Many things I once knew, I have lost
No written record of them, nothing memorized
Even things I once knew by heart
They disappear, like butterflies come winter's first cold breath
Songs I thought up, like ice melting,
Glimmering up as water, to come back later as pictures,
Memories in reading a good book, now knowledgeless that I
    had thought of them far before
Before ever knowing that someone else had known of them as
    well.
Things are lost, some remembered, but some lost to the corners
    of my mind,
Shoved, crammed in like a foot in an outgrown shoe,
Like a tiny figurine jammed into soft mud by a careless child's
    rainboot,
And things I have tried so hard not to forget,
A moments' distraction while memorizing
Stops and all comes unwound
Like hair let out of a braid, or rope tying ship to dock.
The ship floats away, leaving cries of desperation from people
    all around the only thing to remember it by.
A lone memory aboard a ship, leaving
To return? I know not

52

By Ryne

The Mystic Road

By Samuel, at age 14

Traveling down a mystic road,
Walking through the fog, trying to find my way.
Pitfalls and sidetracks to be avoided.
Looking for my destiny.

Traveling down a mystic road
Watching for traps and beasts that lurk in the shadows.
Some people are friends and some are foes.
Trying to find my way.

Traveling down a mystic road,
Guides direct me along my way.
Power and sunshine light the road.
I'm looking forward to what's ahead.

Images

By Erin, at age 14

When I close my eyes, I see darkness
In this darkness I see a crystal ball
In this crystal ball, I see images
In the images, I see people
In these people, I see hatred
In these people, I see anger
In these people, I see fear
Around these people, I see darkness
In this darkness, I see bursts of light
In these bursts of light, I see fire
In this fire, I see families
In these families, I see frightened people
I see these people in my crystal ball
I open my eyes, I can not see my crystal ball
But I still see the images

Summer's End

By Claire, at age 17

The
Season
Of summer
Dies so autumn
Lives.

Over There

By Claire, at age 17

The long ago fallen blossom petals
Still give off aroma strong and fair.
I see that you still smell its scent,
Although you are all the way over there.

Dance of the Sword

By Claire, at age 17

Who will cry for the little girl,
Whose mother has flame-farewelled?
Who will cry for the little girl,
Whose father meets death having felled?
Who will cry for the little boy,
Who is forced to play with mud?
Who will cry for the little boy,
Who has nothing to eat but crud?
Who will cry for the little sister,
Whose brow-stars show slaughter-dew?
Who will cry for the little sister,
Whose tears on her red are new?
The dance of the sword has rolled into town.
The rotten raven harvests form a crown.

The Jury

By Claire, at age 17

A jury loiters.
Hatred walks but the men break.
Poverty prevails.

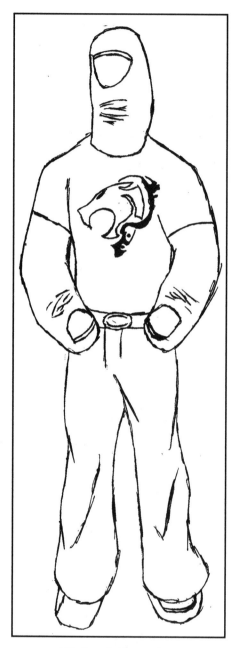

"He's all thumbs"
By Sami

Literal and Concrete Thinking

"When I use a word," Humpty Dumpty said, in rather a scornful tone, "it means just what I choose it to mean – neither more nor less."
– Lewis Carrol, Alice in Wonderland

K ids with Asperger Syndrome want you to say exactly what you mean – after all, *they* do. But the world doesn't always cooperate. We fling around metaphors, similes, idioms ... we have so many artsy ways of making our language less precise! Some kids with Asperger's pick these terms and phrases up easily if parents and teachers explicitly teach what they mean. Some, as you saw in the previous chapter, even become poets themselves. Others struggle with these language issues throughout their lives.

A concrete style of thought can also make it difficult to "read between the lines" and to recognize that there are exceptions to most rules. It can truly be a baffling world out there! But if you're willing to step up as an interpreter, you can help the child with Asperger's learn the language and the laws of the land.

It Never Hurts to Be Cautious

Andrew K, at age 4

One weekend, Andrew spent the night with his great-grandparents. The next day, when the family sat down to their traditional Saturday breakfast of pancakes, Andrew started a new routine. He'd take a bite, stick his fingers in his ears while he chewed and swallowed, then remove his fingers. Then he would take another bite, and repeat the process. Completely befuddled, his mom watched him eat like this for a few minutes and finally asked what in the world he was doing.

Andrew: "Mom, Papa said that if I ate another bite of pancakes, they'd be coming out of my ears!"

One Can Never Be Too Careful

Forrest, at age 2

"Sun is fire, so you have to put lotion on so you don't burn from the sun."

Bunny Hop

Brennan, at age 5

Mom and Brennan were reading the book Lunch Bunnies *by Kathryn Lasky. Bunny Clyde has worried endlessly about his first day of school, especially how to handle the cafeteria line. When lunchtime finally comes, Clyde manages his tray just fine, but he sees his worst nightmare come to life for classmate Rosemary, when she slips on juice and her Jello goes flying. Clyde helps her clean up and realizes that it was really no big deal – his fears were totally out of proportion.*

Brennan: "But Mom, the reason the bunnies drop the food on the floor is because they don't walk, they have to hop."

Cub Scout Rules

Andrew K, in kindergarten

One of the highlights of Andrew's kindergarten year was joining Cub Scouts. At his first pack meeting, the Cub Master was chastising the older Scouts who had been playing in the stalls – not flushing, and not washing their hands. To drive her point home, she said that if she caught any of the boys failing to flush or wash their hands at any Scout function, they wouldn't be allowed to remain in the pack.

The following day, the district had a Cub Fun Day at camp, especially for the new boys. It wasn't long before Andrew had to use the port-a-potty. After an extended wait, his mom finally called in to him, "Is everything OK in there?" A quavering voice answered. "NOOOOOooo ..." and then he started sobbing.

When Mom finally got Andrew to calm down and come out, he told her, "I can't be a Boy Scout any more! I can't flush the toilet!" whereupon he dissolved into tears again.

Trying not to laugh, Mom explained that the Cub Master knows that camp toilets don't flush, but instead, you have to put the lid down. That's how you "flush" toilets at camp.

Andrew slowly calmed down as he processed this information. But then he began looking around furtively, and began sobbing all over again.

Mom: "What now?"

Andrew: "There's no sink!"

No Wonder He Looked Concerned

Rilind, at age 3

One day when Rilind was 3 (before his family found out he had Asperger Syndrome), his mom played with him for a while, until she finally had to sit down and take a break.

Mom: "Boy, Rilind, you sure pooped me out!"

Rilind: (looking confused and concerned) *"I pooped you out?"*

Inquiring Minds Want to Know

Forrest, at age 5

"Mom, are crayons TOXIC? Because I saw a crayon that said 'non-toxic' so I'm guessing that some might be toxic."

You Tell Her!

Breanna, at age 6

Nasty Kid at School: "Get lost!"

Breanna: "I know my way around this school, thank you very much!"

My sister blew her top.

By Allura

Where Else Would You Find a Number?

Khalid, at age 6

Khalid has a superhero obsession. He's come up with 70+ super-heroes of his own (the Blue Blur was the first superhero he ever invented). When he was 6, he went out on a crime-fighting mission.

Khalid: "Mom, after I'm done fighting crime as the Blue Blur, I'll come right back here to this house."

Mom: "OK, that would be great."

Khalid: "But Mom, these mysteries are going to take a long time, so you'll need to be patient. Remember that."

Mom: "OK, I'll try."

Khalid: "I'll find a good phone number for me. How's this? 463-9923?"

Mom: "OK, where'd you find it?"

Khalid: "Calculator."

Little Pitchers

Tamara, at age 8

One day Tamara went to play with a little girl up the street. Tamara recalled her parents' comments that the neighbor's yard looked like a junkyard and their speculation that the inside of their house was probably a mess as well. So, while she was over there, she asked if she could use the phone. And with her friend's mother standing right next to her, she called home and announced:

"Guess what? The house isn't really that bad inside after all!"

Tamara's mom says she and her husband "felt so guilty and ashamed that we NEVER said anything negative about someone else again, at least not in front of Tamara. She had taught us the biggest lesson of all!"

Compliments Come in Many Shapes and Sizes

Duncan, at age 11

"Nana, your butt is pretty fluffy ... but it's a beautiful butt."

Lost, Not Found

Adam A, at age 6

Adam overheard his parents discussing their neighbor, who'd had a miscarriage. Later, he went to his mother with some concerns.

Adam: "Mom, Mrs. Smith is not very smart."

Mom: "Why do you say that?"

Adam: "Well, I heard you tell dad she lost the baby. So if she didn't find it yet, she must not be very smart!"

There's an Explanation for Everything

Graham, at age 10

"Actually, magic is just misunderstood science or technology."

Park It

Alex, at age 3

From an early age, Alex was very interested in how to operate a car. Whenever his family went for a drive, he'd ask what gear they were in and why. So he quickly learned that "R" on the console meant REVERSE, that "D" meant DRIVE, etc.

One day, Mom and Alex were having one of their typical power struggles over getting ready for school and getting into the car. Mom thought the battle was over when she finally got Alex buckled into his car seat. But as she started backing out of the garage, Alex started fussing.

Alex: "But Mom, I just want P! I want you to stay in PARK!"

Party Line

Russell, at age 13

Russell and his mom were headed out the door to a party – one that he didn't particularly want to attend.

Russell: "Didn't you say that I was invited to go to this party?"

Mom: "Yes, you were invited."

Russell: "Doesn't it mean when you're *invited* to something that you have a choice whether or not to go?"

Mom couldn't figure out how to argue with that!

No Need for Overkill

Forrest, at age 2

Forrest went on the potty, and afterwards Mom helped him wash BOTH hands.

Forrest: (Somewhat annoyed) "Hey, I only touched the potty with ONE hand!"

Just Checking

Forrest, at age 3

One day Forrest accidentally slipped off his stool at lunchtime. He wasn't badly hurt, but he asked his mom, just to be sure:

"Mommy, check if I have a black eye ... I still have two blue eyes?"

Memaw's Passing

Chase, at age 9

It can sometimes be tempting to think that a child who has a very concrete style of thought is somehow missing out. But this story illustrates how that concrete approach can be a source of comfort during difficult times.

Shortly after Chase was diagnosed with Asperger Syndrome, his great-grandmother passed away. Mom let Chase decide for himself how involved he wanted to be with the memorial. He went to the funeral home once, where his grandmother tried to get him to touch "Memaw," because he has always "touched" his world to completely comprehend what his eyes were seeing. Chase would not touch Memaw, but he did touch her dress.

Chase showed no emotion at the funeral home, even though he had truly loved Memaw. He chose not to go to the funeral, because he said he didn't want to miss "treasure box day" at school. Mom did not force the issue, although many family members were appalled that she would "shelter" him or force him to forgo his final good-byes. But Mom did what most of us do in difficult situations with our kids: "I just played it by ear."

Memaw's death was devastating to Chase's mother, and she cried a lot. About a week after the funeral, Chase was finally ready to talk to her about it in his own way.

Chase: "Mom, why do you cry so much?"

Mom: "Because my heart hurts and I am going to miss her."

Chase: "Well Mom, it is like this ... You are born and you live your life, then when God is ready, he calls you home ... and you die. But you go home. Why be sad about going home?"

With that, he was done with the conversation. Mom was amazed at his statement, since their family is not religious, and Chase had never been to church or had any bible lessons.

About a week after that conversation, Chase sat up in bed in the middle of the night and called out.

Chase: "Mom! MOM!!"

Mom: "What, Chase?"

Chase: "Mom, it is a good thing that we gave Gizmo (his dog) to Memaw and Pappaw when we moved into the new house."

Mom: "Why is that?" (Thinking that she personally had really been missing that dog since they moved.)

Chase: "Well, Pappaw has Gizmo and Petey (his great-grand-parents' poodle), so he won't be lonely with Memaw gone."

Chase then lay back down and went to sleep. He has refused to ever discuss Memaw's death again. With that last sentence, he felt he had put the issue to rest.

People sometimes think that kids with Asperger Syndrome don't have a sense of humor. Not true! Many kids with Asperger's adore slapstick comedy, comic strips, word puns, and more. But sometimes their literal thinking or their difficulty interpreting personal interactions prevents them from "getting" a joke.

Dad Tries to Tell a Joke

David, at age 6

Dad: "Hey, David, what's the difference between a mailbox and a toilet?"

David: "Dad, there's lots of differences!"

Dad: "No, just say 'I don't know, what?' What's the difference between a mailbox and a toilet?"

David: "OK, only one flushes."

Dad: "No, just say 'What?' What's the difference between a mailbox and a toilet?"

David: "You should only put your mail in one of them."

Dad: "No, this is a joke. You're just supposed to say 'I don't know, what?' What's the difference between a mailbox and a toilet? Now say 'What?'"

David: "There's only water in one of them."

Dad: "No, I'm telling you, this is a joke! When I say, 'What's the difference between a mailbox and a toilet,' you're supposed to say, 'I don't know. What?' What's the difference between a mailbox and a toilet? Now say 'What?' Say it! Say it!"

David: *(with great exasperation)* "What?"

Dad: "Boy, remind me never to give you any letters to mail for me! Ha ha!"

David: "Was I supposed to mail letters?"

Grateful for Small Favors

Kim, at age 15

(After riding in the back of the family minivan for 45 minutes while her older sister got a driving lesson from Mom)

Kim: "Thank God, we're back on dry land!"

A Sign

Noah, at age 6

When Noah, who has high-functioning autism, was 6, his family was getting ready for a garage sale. Noah found the stack of signs, ready to be posted. He picked one up, so his mom told him, "Noah, put that sign up."

Noah raised the sign above his head and began marching around in a circle, singing: "The sign is up! The sign is up!"

Lullaby

By Forrest, at age 2

Rock-a-bye baby on the treetop ...
When the wind blows, the cradle breaks,
But when the wind doesn't blow, the cradle doesn't break.

He is really on the ball.

By Allura

Questions From a Martian Scientist

Josi, at age 10

Josi's mom says, "It can be hard to understand what motivates Earthlings when you are a Martian Scientist (her daughter with high-functioning autism). It can also be hard to understand the difference between sentient and nonsentient beings. But I'll give her credit for continuing to research the answers." Here are a few examples of recent questions from Josi:

- Why do kids sometimes cry when their parents scold them?
- Do fires know when campers leave so that they can try to get outside of the campfire?
- Why is murder worse than robbery?
- Why do girls like fashion?
- Was I funny?
- Was I good at being sarcastic?
- (about any undesirable behavior from another person) Is he mean?
- What does it mean if his eyebrows are down but he is smiling?
- Will you love me even after you're dead?

Jeepers!

David, at age 4

At age 4, David's favorite game was "scaring" his dad, who would usually provide a very goofy, over-the-top response. One day David decided to jump out from behind the chair to scare his dad:

David: "ROAR!!"

Dad: "Arghhh!!! ... Geez, David, you scared the bejeepers out of me!"

David: (aghast) "Daaaaaaaad!"

Dad: "What?"

David: "You know!"

Dad: "I know what?"

David: "Men don't have bejeepers!"

Dad: "What do you think bejeepers are?"

David: "Aren't they the things ladies have on their chests? The things with moles?"

Like Father, Like Son

Matt, at age 12

Dad got home from work and reacted rather melodramatically when he learned that Mom had not made supper for him.

Dad: "I might as well go throw myself on the railway track!"

Johnny: "Mom, he's not really going to do that is he? You know how literal dad is!"

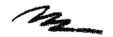

Tools of the Trade

Forrest, at age 3

"Builders use CONSTRUCTION paper."

By Riland

Relationships

"Even the utmost goodwill and harmony and practical kindness are not sufficient for Friendship, for Friends do not live in harmony merely, as some say, but in melody."

– Henry David Thoreau

C hildren with Asperger Syndrome tend to be fiercely loyal to the ones they love – their family, pets, special teachers, and, once they make them, their friends. But making friends can be one of their biggest challenges growing up.

Children make friends by playing together. By the time they start elementary school, most neurotypical children have naturally progressed through the various stages of social play:
- from solitary play,
- to parallel play (doing the same activity independently, but side by side with a playmate),
- to associative play (still playing independently, but sharing, taking turns, and talking to other children),
- to cooperative play (playing together with a common goal, each child taking a different role or responsibility).

But for a child with Asperger Syndrome, that progression doesn't come so naturally. Cooperative play, and even associative play, requires good social skills and flexibility – areas where a child with Asperger's lags behind. Early on, the child may not even realize that his relationships with other kids are lacking; she may happily refer to any child who says hello to her as her "best friend." But as the child matures, she may begin to better understand the concept of friendship, and even long for true friends, but not know how to go about making them.

So does that mean a child with Asperger Syndrome is destined for a lonely life? No! Social skills – taking turns, asking others about themselves, etc. – can be taught. And while the child may not be able to play cooperatively by age 5, that doesn't mean she can't learn to do so eventually.

Most kids with Asperger Syndrome will not grow up to be smooth-talking salespeople or social butterflies. Small talk may never be their forté (just as it isn't for lots of folks). But once they master some basic social skills, there will be other children who can see through the awkwardness to spot the amazing kids they are – enthusiastic, brilliant, and, yes, a bit quirky.

Often, the tightest bonds form with kids who share their special interests. When the child who has memorized every line of every episode of *Dragonball Z* finally meets another child who loves the Japanese cartoon just as obsessively, it's a pretty magical moment. Suddenly, he has someone who speaks the same language. And he realizes he's not alone.

By Zak

My Parents

By Evelyn, at age 8

My parents are as sweet as candy
Because the taste of candy is easy to
love and so are my parents.

No Mincing of Words

By Duncan, at age 11

"Teacher is one cruel woman. All she does is torture kids!"

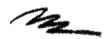

Notable

By Andrew S, at age 9

Andrew was playing Nintendo with his older brother and a neighbor when he accidentally erased one of the games off the neighbor's memory card. After the boys got mad at him, Andrew wrote them a note. The grammar might be less than perfect, but it definitely expressed his feelings clearly:

> "Jesse and Kirby,
>
> You guys are giving a bad day and it's all your fault.
> I am swinging on the swing.
> I am sad that I'm sorry about erased Kirby's game.
> You guys don't trust me.
>
> – Andrew. "

Then he drew a sad face with tears.

Different Kinds of People

By David, at age 9

Mean
cruel, unkind
hurting, scaring, humiliating
words, actions, words, actions
helping, supporting, trusting
friendly, respectful
Kind

Teacher

By Rina, at age 9

Mrs. Reed is as exciting
as a good book.
Her teaching is a real adventure.

Why Mrs. Humphrey Is the Best

By Khalid, at age 8

Khalid had a lot to say about one of his favorite aides, Mrs. Humphrey:

"Know why Mrs. Humphrey is the best? Because she says she'll save my stick and she really does!"

"Mrs. Humphrey said she believed me ... Finally, someone believes me!"

"Mrs. Humphrey liked my present better than anyone else did because she got the most excited!"

"The best thing about Mrs. Humphrey is she never lies."

That Crazy College

By Christopher, at age 7

That crazy college
its full of knowledge.
but people are mean
because
I'm in between
that crazy college
its full of knowledge.

Written while Christopher was taking a summer writing class through the Center for the Gifted at a local college.

Little Brother

Lars, at age 7

Lars one day commented about his little brother:

"He's the best entertainment a boy could ask for!"

Comfort from Avery

When Avery was 3 years old, his uncle was killed. On a day when the loss was hitting his mother particularly hard, Avery found her sitting on the couch. He came up behind her, hugged her neck, and started to rock back and forth with her. Then he started to sing this sweet little song:

"Hush little mommy don't you cry, Avery's going to make you a Stinky Pie!"

Mom says she almost died laughing as she rolled off the couch with a giggling Avery in her arms. "I will never forget how he brightened up my otherwise dark day!"

Daddy's Baby

Forrest, at age 2

Forrest was potty-trained when his baby sister was born. One day, he had an "accident" for no apparent reason.

Dad: "Forrest, why'd that happen?"

Forrest: "When I tinkle in my pants, I'm still Daddy's baby."

Brothers

By Jimmy, at age 9

Jimmy
brilliant, resourceful
thinking, answering, correcting
boy, son, boy, son
talking, laughing, jumping
playful, humorous
Sandy

Love Is You

By Khalid, at age 9

Love is something you cannot see.
Love is you, my sweet mommy.

Happy Father's Day, Popeye

By Khalid, at age 6

Father
kind, active
jogging, hiding, running
wrestle, football, basketball, patient
swimming, playing, loving
nice, cool
popeye

Happy Father's Day!

Love, Khalid

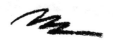

My Friend

By Robyn, at age 9

David is as perfect as a peony
that has just bloomed

Father

By Khalid, at age 7

Funny voices you make.
Amazing jokes you tell.
Terrific mind for thinking.
Helps me when needed.
Ever-lasting happiness.
Remarkable grip when mad.

Love, Khalid

My Mom

By Khalid, at age 6

My mom is a diamond that shines the brightest.
My mom is the Queen of queens.
My mom is gold no one can find.
My mom is loving, helping and truthful.

Love, Khalid

PS: you're the best!!!

Happy Valentine's, Mother

By Khalid, at age 7

Love is like the wind blowing kisses.
Love is something you can't see.
Love is very warm.
Love is like money.
Love is very big.
Love is very bright.
Love is you mom.

Love, Khalid

Sister

By Abigail, at age 11

(Upon big sis returning to college after winter break)

I had never seen
How she had grown.
I never noticed,
But now I think how things will be,
Without Her.

Me and My Sister Lena

By Anna C, at age 11

Me and my sister Lena love to do wonderful things together to show we are friends and sisters together.

- Have holiday parties with our pretend friends.
- Have outdoor celebrations with our pretend relatives and friends, and dolls, and family.
- Have balls.
- Pretend to go exploring at night (sneaking into a room we shouldn't go into!).
- Share visions and images of pretend places.
- Build pretend shopping centers.
- Coloring maps of the U.S. together
- Share interests in states and World Geography and countries.
- Watch license plates from different states (We've seen Alaska, and Lena's seen a Hawaii!). (We haven't seen Wyoming and North Dakota yet!).
- Do festivals together, celebrating countries, and states!
- Make potholders for our pretend friends, relatives, dolls and family.
- Write letters to our pretend friends.
- Put on plays together (*Cinderella, Sound of Music, Little Women*).
- Teach our dolls classes.

- Get together with our dolls, family, relatives, and friends.

- Pretend to go into colorful rooms when exploring at night.

- Make cards and other special gifts for our family, dolls, relatives and friends.

- Describe imaginary places (like a place called Magic City) me and Lena have imagined.

- Talk with our family, relatives, friends and dolls.

- Plan to go to special places to visit our family, relatives, dolls and friends.

- Have fun together no matter what!

Happiness Is ... A Family

Forrest, at age 2

"I love having a family with you."

My Little Sister

By Bridget, at age 9

My little sister is one of the best friends anyone could know. She is the greatest little sister ever! It is always a joy to see her. She is so cute. I love her more than almost anything in the world, and it would break my heart if she died. She is smart and nice and she has a lot of ideas for amusement. Now I feel like we are skipping through all the flowers or getting married to each other even if we are girls.

P.S. Her smile is cute too.

Love Is a Many-Splendored Thing

Forrest, at age 2 (during his Bob The Builder *phase)*

"Mommy, I have to tell you something ... I love building. Mommy, I have to tell you something else ... I love you."

Metaphor Family

By Rina, at age 11

My mom is a tulip poplar; she is not lazy and watches over us.
My dad is a redwood; he is rough on us and barely cares about
    anyone in his environment.
Orli is a holly tree; she is aggressive and invades people's spaces
    with her prickly leaves.
Noah and I are Japanese red maples; we provoke each other but
    still get along well.

Gizmo

By David, at age 10

My dog Gizmo is the best dog on Earth. He is as perfect as
heaven itself. I spend a lot of my free time either playing
with him or cuddling with him. To cuddle with Gizmo is like
lying down in a soft, furry pillow. In fact, just being around
him is like having all of your problems washed down the
drain. When I first got him though, I didn't appreciate how
good he was. But soon I learned to love him. Now, he is as
important to me as the air that I breathe.

Animal Friends

By Robyn, at age 9

Animals
give pleasure
to aching hearts
on days that seem against you

By Andrew

Please Bring Her Back

By Connor, at age 11
(Dedicated to Cocoa and Nutmeg,
His Loving Companions)

I had two young dogs,
Then one passed away.
The other one stayed,
And whined away.
She cried all night,
And whined all day.
I saw her eyes,
She wanted to say,
Can you please
Bring her back.
That was all,
She would say.
Then I cried,
all night and day.
The misery in her,
Was also in me.
Then the day came,
For her to go.
But before she left me,
Her eyes said it all.
She wanted her back.
That was all she could say.
But the thing that she wanted,
The only thing she wanted.
Nobody could give.

A Little Piece of Heaven

Warren, at age 12

As any Asperger parent knows, friendships and desires can be bittersweet. Toward the end of sixth grade, Warren started hinting that he liked a classmate named Orelis. Mom tried to give him advice from a woman's perspective, but Warren was too shy to let Orelis know he liked her. His only communication with her was one of harmless teasing when he banded together with two of his buddies.

One day after school, Warren got in the car and informed Mom that Orelis was now going out with Anthony, a boy at school who came from a "rich" family. Mom tried to soothe his disappointment and redirect his thoughts.

Mom:　　"Well, remember, money will not buy anyone's way into a heaven."

Warren:　"Anthony has Orelis and she's a little piece of heaven!"

To Weave the Impossible Dream

By Dylan, at age 15

To dream the impossible dream
I have found a place without pretense,
where all dare dream the impossible dream,
and the dream, dreamed by all, is no longer a dream,
And into being we play this world
and give it essence with our love and play,
For of what world are these not the soul?
And what mortal heart has felt not this hole?

To fight the unbeatable foe
When the time comes for battle with my "foes" I'll dance
and give not a care to who's the victor.

To love pure and chaste from afar
And as I see the way of this place,
yes,
I love pure,
and yes,
chaste too is my love,
as I lean on your shoulder
and feel your warmth.

Oh yes, I used to love from afar,
longing for touch tempered by fear
of what a touch might mean,
and how it might be taken.

But as I watched
the way you touched
slowly I realized,
and relaxed,
and am relaxing into
the arms of those who have given me
the two great gifts of the playmate.

So now,
as you hold me so near,
I feel your warmth without guilt or fear.

**To try when my arms are too weary to reach the unreach-
able star,**
And the dark clouds of fear part
revealing so many loving star-like planets,
but then one night the full moon rises in splendor like a
noon-day sun
or so it seems until I am caught in this fallen star's arms.

Like an angelic balrog dancing with colored cloth,
this goddess, Calsophia,
as our embrace fades and ends,
my heel I turn but my heart looks back.
And her scarf wraps round my heart.
Seizing it yet warming it
Without even knowing what she has caught
wrapped in that cloth
Which hopes she will notice it
Unwrap it and hold it,
Its skin bare against hers,
Basking in her warmth.

To right the unrightable wrong
which feels so right in my heart,
yet so shy am I that through the shadows I dart
and afraid to show my soul
instead in shadows hide it.

But to live in the shadows
is to be shadowed
and a hidden soul
is one you Hyde.

I have found love.
Now I must lose fear.

So I'll try with my last ounce of courage, to reach the un-reachable star,
To fling open the doors of my soul,
So I can breathe the air of this loving world.
A world which opens itself to those
who open themselves to it.

(Bolded lines are derived from the lyrics of "To Dream the Impossible Dream" from Man of La Mancha)

By Samantha

Special Interests

"Only one who devotes himself to a cause with his whole strength and soul can be a true master. For this reason mastery demands all of a person."

– Albert Einstein

One of the most distinguishing characteristics of individuals with Asperger Syndrome is an all-encompassing interest. Lots of children love Pokémon or Thomas the Tank Engine, but few can match the sheer volume of information a child with Asperger's will have memorized about his favorite topic. Simply amassing facts about a pet subject can be a source of great joy for a child with Asperger Syndrome.

Some children with Asperger's develop interests that are very unique; examples range from deep fat fryers to game show hosts. Others have interests similar to those of their neurotypical peers (e.g., video games, baseball scores, horses, computers, cartoons) – just on a much grander scale. Topics that often seem to grab the interest of kids with Asperger's include science, transportation (especially trains and train schedules), electronics, computers, and animals.

Unfortunately, some children can be so preoccupied with their special interest that they resist being taught about ... well, anything else. When this is a problem, savvy teachers first adapt lessons to include the child's interest ("If Calvin threw 12 snowballs at Suzie and 13 at Hobbes, how many snowballs did he throw altogether?") and then build on that interest ("Today we're each going to research a mammal. Hmmm, I wonder if Calvin has a favorite mammal? Tigers? Great, David, why don't you do your report on tigers."). Some of the poetry and essays included in this section were written by kids who are typically reluctant writers but were coaxed into participating because they could expound on their favorite subjects.

Anna was very into stars when she wrote this poem, but Mom says she was more interested in them as toys than as astral bodies. Several years later, Anna still has her limited collection of five assorted star dolls – star "stuffed animal" type toys with faces.

Stars

By Anna C, at age 9-1/2

They are little faces
With squinty eyes.
They curtsy in
the evening sky
And nod to
planets
singing by.

David's first-grade reading teacher told his mom one day that he wouldn't – or couldn't – write even the simplest third-person narrative. That weekend, Mom asked David to make up a story about Spider-Man, and promised that she would type it as he dictated. This is the result.

Intergalactic Spider-Man: The Origin

By David, at age 7

Just after Mingle – the Spider-Man of 2099 – dies, the Spider-Man of nowadays appears. He discovers that his time machine breaks down, and he is trapped inside the year 2099. He discovers the alien symbiote that he once wore from the Alien Symbiote story. It seems that Venom discovers an even stronger costume, so he goes to the top of the church tower and uses the bells to blast the symbiote off of him. The symbiote decides that Spider-Man is better than Brock, even when he first met Brock. So he absorbs all that Spidey tells about himself into his abilities and once again he bonds with Spider-Man. Spidey does not want, though, to go back into the past. He wants to tour some of the planets of 2099 before he goes back into the past. *And so begins the series of Intergalactic Spider-Man!*

First Trip – The Moon. Part 1

As Spidey's space ship approaches the moon of 2099, Spidey discovers a strange fog and thinks in his mind "Hmmm, that looks like the fog that comes from Mysterio's boots." Then Spidey instantly discovers "Wait a second, that IS Mysterio!"

Spidey jumps out of his space ship so quickly that it clears the fog and he manages to find Mysterio. But Mysterio manages to turn himself into a giant inside a room with no exit with special power sources on his knees, hips, and nipples. He manages to raise his arms, causing Spidey's spider sense to tingle. Spidey wonders why his spider sense starts to tingle. Then suddenly a rolling thing with spikes starts rolling around. Spidey manages to destroy the power sources on the ground on Mysterio's knees. Suddenly an energy source coming from the ground lifts him up to Mysterio's head. He discovers that lasers have grown in place of his power sources. By *thwipping* the lasers twice with his webbing, it takes them out.

But Mysterio still has one more trick up his sleeve. He brings powerful energy moving around his globe and suddenly his globe turns red and electricity makes the floors below that electrical. But by *thwipping* his globe, Mysterio suddenly screams in pain and as he gets lights, he whirls around getting smaller and smaller until he gets to normal size. END OF CHAPTER ONE. SEE CHAPTER TWO – KRAVEN ON MARS!

Chapter 2 – KRAVEN ON MARS!

Spidey's starship called The Spider Disk swung through space until it reached Mars. Then Spidey noticed, "Hmmmm, I know that there's supposed to be aliens on Mars, but smoke? Aliens aren't supposed to have the technology to create smoke!" But there IS smoke! Spidey gets out of the Spider Disk and swung out and suddenly his spider sense tingles and he uses his spider speed to avoid the net with heavy balls on the tip of it. He reaches down to

earth and he thinks "Am I going mad? There are two cheetahs right in front of me!" Suddenly Spidey spots an old
foe, "Kraven, what are you doing here?!" But Kraven just
responds, "Finally, the prey is mine!" And Spidey's spider
sense allows him to just make it through the galaxy of lasers
fired by Kraven's eyes on the lion's mane over his neck.

Spidey manages to get the close up, but suddenly "Wham!"
and Spidey's nearly out! Then Spidey is finally defeated with
one blow. Once he wakes up, he is right in between Kraven
and the core of Mars. Just as he's about to throw Spidey
into the core, Spidey manages to snap the titanium chains
made by Kraven and, in the process, he accidentally knocked
Kraven toward the core. Kraven managed to dodge the core,
but his arm was accidentally injured by scraping across the
core, and people around the world are wondering if Kraven
will ever hunt again.

End chapter two. NEXT TIME, CHAPTER 3 – ELECTRO
ON PLUTO!

Five years later, David no longer needs to dictate. Thanks to a fabulous teacher, and a lot of hard work, he can now write by hand or keyboard. In fact, he's become a straight-A student. David can write about any subject he's assigned, but when he's writing for fun(!), superheroes are still a favorite topic. Here's a description of a new superhero he's thought up.

Radiator

By David, at age 11

Secret identity: David M., high school student

Origin: When on a field trip to a nuclear power plant, David wanders off, disobeying teachers. He discovers a secret government project to create a combination of all forms of radiation, thus supplying infinite energy. However, due to the massive amount of radiation, it becomes unstable. The containment area runs out of energy, resulting in a massive explosion. David is caught in the explosion, causing massive infusion of super-powers. Designs the costume, decides to help people in need, yadda, yadda, yadda, you get the drill.

Powers: Super-strength, super-speed, flight, invulnerability, radioactive energy blasts, enhanced intelligence, x-ray vision, infrared vision, telekinesis, and limited molecular manipulation, such as change the temperature of something albeit heat vision/freeze breath. He can also bend things to a limited degree, and temporarily become intangible, but it takes much of his energy. When the explosion happened, unknown to everyone but David, a capsule was created, the finished combination of the radiation, and that is what replenishes his powers. He can also use an energy shield that protects him from everything, even radiation and electricity, and it works on organic matter. However, it only stays up for 30 seconds, and if it stays up the whole 30 seconds, he loses his powers for 30 seconds. Also, he can create a nuclear explosion, size depending on how big he wants it to be, but this drains all his power, even if he's just recharged.

Weaknesses: If he goes 14 days without recharging, he will lose his powers until he recharges. Any form of radioactivity other then the combined radiation will drain his powers into it. If exposed for too long, will lose all powers, but will not harm him. Any power drained into it will be permanently drained from him until he recharges. Also, if anyone comes near the radiation that has sucked his energy, for up to three days the person gains all his powers for however long before the power vanishes. He is not invulnerable to electricity, and it hurts and harms him just as much as us. He can also control it normally from a distance of 300 feet or more, but any closer and he loses more and more control over it. Up close, he is powerless against it. It can kill him easily, and he may be more vulnerable to it then regular humans.

"Grace the Vampire Slayer"
By Grace

Colin, who has autism, wrote the following story about Sonic the Hedgehog – a popular video game and comic book character. While Colin wrote it all in one paragraph, we've broken it up to make it easier to read. Otherwise, the story is unedited.

Sonic's Christmas Carol

By Colin "Oxide" R, at age 8

Once upon time, there was a hedgehog named Sonic. Do you want to hear a story about a Christmas Carol? Sure. The story has three heroes, Knuckles, Sonic, and Tails who stop 3 ghosts and one evil witch and the thunder goblins.

Our story begins on a silent night. All hedgehogs and family are enjoying a Christmas party. They are singing a song about when we hear a Christmas Carol. Eggman was pretending to be Scrooge. He steals things.

Sonic and his friends work hard every year, but now Actrabell, the evil hedgehog, has arrived. She has a machine, the giant red cymbal. Actrabell is going to destroy Christmas.

A moment later, Sonic, Knuckles, and Tails will be the three ghosts: the ghost of Christmas Past, the ghost of Christmas Present, and the ghost of Christmas Future.

A few seconds later, Eggman is eating popcorn and Eggman hates Christmas. Eggman was watching the Dr. Eggman on Live on television. Now Sonic, the Jacob Marley appears. Jacob Marley is telling about a great Eggman, but Eggman couldn't make Jacob Marley disappear. Jacob told him about three ghosts from the story for ringing the bell. The ghost challenge will begin. Now the bell rang and Jacob Marley said, "Oh, it's time for the first ghost; there are three spirits" said Jacob Marley. "Farewell, Eggman." Eggman said, "No ghosts, you fool."

Jacob Marley grabbed Eggman and took him to the first ghost. Eggman said, "Are you Knuckles?" Knuckles said, "No, I'm not Knuckles. I'm the ghost of Christmas Past." "Now, come along", said Knuckles. So, Eggman looked at it and said, "It's my mom." So, your teleportion took you to Eggman's special home. Now, Eggman sings about why did we know, but I dreamed about the naughty man. Eggman hates Christmas and he tossed Knuckles into a deep snow.

Now, it the bell rings again and Jacob Marley said, "It's time for the second ghost, Eggman." Jacob Marley grabs Eggman again and takes him to the second ghost. Eggman saw the bright light and said, "Are you Tails?" Tails said, "No, I'm not Tails. I'm the ghost of Christmas Present. Come Along." They travel to Eggman's place. "It's my partner," said Dr. Eggman. Now, Eggman's partner said, "I sing about thinking about a Christmas Day."

Eggman travels to another place and sees a new pet named Tommy. Eggman said, "Cool. This place looks familiar." Tails said, "Do you think the pet's name is Tommy?" Eggman said, "Yes." Tommy was dizzy and broke the plate and Santa will not like it. Eggman says, "I'm happy. I'm sad. I'm sorry Tails. I'm sorry. You're the ghost of Christmas Present." Eggman says again, "I'm sorry pet. I'm sorry pet. I'm sorry pet."

Eggman is watching the channel again about Eggman on Live. Jacob Marley said, "There's one more spirit left. Hear the bell. Here's the third ghost, the ghost of Christmas Future." Eggman sees a comic book and says, "Cool," but the bell rings again. Jacob Marley said, "It's the third ghost. It's time for ghost number three."

Jacob Marley grabs Eggman a third time. Eggman travels to the comic book world. Eggman sees him and says, "Are you Sonic?" "No, I'm not Sonic. I'm the ghost of Christmas Future." Sonic sings the song about Fix the World.

Eggman travels to Tommy's place again. Eggman looks at the clock telling time and Eggman said, "It's 12:30, Oh no, Actrabell is going to slam the giant Red Cymbal." Now, Eggman makes Tommy stop, and it doesn't work. Eggman gives up and said, "Nooooooooooooo. I'm sorry ghost of Christmas Future. I'm sorry." Sonic said, "Why did you know a thing? Why did you know an action? Try that figure you are."

Jacob Marley said, "That's the end of the ghost challenge. Good-bye." That's the end of Eggman on Live. Eggman had a good dream.

Now, Actrabell was back and said, "It's time for your de-light!" Sonic says, "It's a nightmare. We must stop Actrabell for good."

Eggman and Eggman's partner travel to Actrabell's place. Actrabell activates the generator and destroys Christmas. Trees turn into monsters. Ghosts turn into nightmares.

Actrabell said, "Yes, Christmas was ruined and destroyed!" Eggman says, "No. No. No."

Sonic, Knuckles, and Tails said, "What did you think you action figures have to worry about. We had trouble with this yesterday. A good man is like you, friend."

Eggman jumps to the electric rope and Eggman said, "This is from Tommy." The red cymbal was destroyed and Christmas is saved.

Actrabell said, "Grrrr, why you!"

Anybell, the angel hedgehog, says, "You saved Christmas! Now, I am going to stop Actrabell."

It snowed and snowed and snowed and defeated Actrabell. Christmas was saved again!

It snowed in the town of a silent night and Eggman said, "Ho ... Ho ... Ho ... Merry Christmas!" He gave all things back to the hedgehogs and families.

That's the end of the story. Do you want to hear it again? Good. "Ahhh, gee," said Sonic and they all lived happily ever after. The End.

When Samuel was 7, his class was given an assignment to write about their community, using all five senses in the description. Samuel didn't want to write about his neighborhood. He wanted to write about his passion – the local wildlife reserve. So with a little help from Mom, he figured out a way to make it work.

My Community: The Sepulveda Basin Wildlife Refuge

By Samuel V, grade 2

My favorite community is the Sepulveda Basin Wildlife Refuge. As soon as we get out of the car, I feel the warm sun on a hot day or the cold wind on a cloudy day. Some days we can smell freshly cut grass.

My favorite time of day at the refuge is morning. We sit quietly, eating warm Egg McMuffins and drinking creamy hot chocolate. We sit on a warm blanket to protect us from the cold, hard bench. The mist as it rises off the lake looks like something out of a fairy tale. Everything looks and smells fresh.

The Canada geese are floating on the water. Then, all at once, the geese start taking off in groups going to the grass on the opposite shore. It's like they all have to be at the office by 8:00. We always know when they're going to take off because they start honking.

My second favorite time of day there is sunset. First, the pelicans do their dinner dance. They go into a tight group somewhere on the lake. All at once, they tip their heads underwater with their rear ends sticking straight up in the air. Then they pop back up with a fish for dinner.

Then the cormorants do a bedtime dance. They fly into the trees on the island to rest for the night. They are usually silent, so all we hear are their wings beating. Sometimes, though, we can hear a loud snap followed by a splash. This happens when a branch breaks and a cormorant falls into the lake.

Lastly, when it is completely dark, off in the distance we can hear honking. The Canada geese, announcing their arrival, hit the water with a splash.

The evening show over, we head for home. Along the way, we stop at the ramp to check for catfish feasting on algae. We climb into the car while listening to croaking frogs and chirping crickets.

By Anna G

Talk about putting a special interest to good use! Kevin's mom says he is obsessed with movies and movie trivia. From the time he was little, he has always wanted to watch videos, so his parents started telling him that he could watch the movie if he wrote a review of it afterward. Well, Mom and Dad's scheme paid off better than they'd ever imagined. Kevin became the "kid movie reviewer" for the local paper. He reviews all of the G- and PG-rated movies (and King Kong, *which was PG-13, but he begged to do it).*

The King of All Movies

By Kevin T, at age 11

Move over, *Lion King,* there's a new ape in town!
This is no *Mighty Joe Young.* This is more incredible than *The Incredibles.* More swinging than *Spider-Man.* More gigantic than *George of the Jungle!* More terrific than *Tarzan!* It's the one, the only, KING KONG!!!

Carl (Jack Black) is a movie producer with a wild mind for films. When he hears the CEO is planning to fire him, he slips away to a ship that will take him to the destination of his next film, *Skull Island.* Everything's going the way it's supposed to. Carl has got a crew, a beautiful female (Naomi Watts), a writer (Adrien Brody) and an actor to do the stunts (Kyle Chandler). No problem, right? Wrong. Once they get on the island, the native people who live there don't take too kindly to the crew. They attack the crew members and later steal Ann, Jack's female, to offer as a sacrifice to Kong.

Once Carl and the crew go into the jungle to search for Ann, they battle dinosaurs, giant snails, and roaches. Kong is busy saving Ann from three dinosaurs and ripping one's jaw open, which I found very sick. They finally rescue Ann, find Kong, and chloroform him by throwing a bottle of the stuff into his eye. They then put him on a ship and take him to New York.

Then it's a love story between female and ape. King Kong is such a hero he saves Ann three times. In one scene in New York, Kong is playing with Ann on the ice in Central Park. Basically he is ice skating on his behumpus. My mom thought it was romantic when they were playing on the ice, but I liked it when the ice exploded as the military shot a gun at Kong. From my perspective, violence rocks, but romance makes me want to barf.

This movie has the kind of violence you see in *Jurassic Park*, but it's funny in some ways, too. When Carl offers a native child some chocolate, he violently grabs Carl's arm and bites him. I had to hide behind my mom's scarf when the natives were offering Ann to Kong, because if you see the natives you'll get nightmares for the rest of your life (or maybe a week). Cover up!

I think it stunk that they made King Kong into a show animal. He seemed human, just like your regular everyday Robert De Niro. I'm not sure who Robert De Niro is, but Kong looked like the kind of guy who should be named Robert De Niro. Will Kong ever escape New York City? Will Ann marry Kong? Will Kong return to his island home?

I gave this movie five stars because it was so good my mom didn't even want to leave her seat to go to the bathroom. Hint: Don't drink a giganto Sprite.

Although he's gifted in math, English has always been more of a challenge for Sean. So when he was required to write a poem using assonance, consonance, and alliteration, he tackled the assignment by laying it out like an equation.

Gamers

By Sean, at age 14

Intelligent, creative,
Strategic and tactical
Using computers or game consoles
Anyone and everyone –
who be game savvy
The great equalizer
A nerd can pwn* people that are stronger

Button mashing
Consuming copious quantities of caffeine
to stay active all night
FFA (or free for alls)
Or team battles
Fingers fly at such a rapid speed
It's as if they have a mind of their own

Great genres of games
Multiple categories within each one
So many things limit playing time
Respect when you pass a level
Honor mixed with disappointment
when the game is over …

* *pwn is a gamer's term. Pronounced "pone," it means to beat an opponent so badly that he or she feels disgraced.*

My Adventure Inside a Computer Game

By Russell, at age 12

I was playing my favorite game, *Where in Space Is Carmen Sandiego*, when I pushed the button to get my warrant. The screen twirled and sucked me inside. I was in outer space, floating. When the gravity increased, I fell and landed on Halley's comet.

Then I jumped off and landed on Neptune. Then I saw the Acme probe floating by with a warrant for Kit Incaboodle. Then I saw a suction cup monster, and I grabbed it. I put it in my bag. I saw Kit Incaboodle. I jumped on it, beat it, punched it, and tied it up. The Acme probe gave me a ride and grabbed the V.I.L.E. henchperson. When we reached the jail, the computer spit me back out. "But the suction cup monster?" I wondered. I opened my bag, and it was gone.

The end.

A Speech About Kittens

By Russell, at age 12

My name is Russell L. I would like to give a speech about kittens.

The reason is I like them, and it's important for everyone to understand why. There are many different kinds of cats. And everyone should own a cat instead of a dog.

Cats are better than Dogs.

Cats are clean, quiet, don't go on walks, and don't stink.

Dogs are the opposite.

Cats come in many breeds, Manx, Persian, calico, Siamese, angora, and Himalayan. Always change their litter and feed them. I like jungle cats cause they have round ears.

So ... In conclusion, since there are more cats than dogs who need homes,

Go to your local animal shelter and adopt one.

Puzzling Thoughts

By Russell, at age 12

Hello Puzzle Fans out there. Are you bored with the same day-to-day schedule? Yes? Well, I ... Russell L. ... have the perfect idea. Did you know that there are lots and lots of puzzles out there for all ages? Not first graders, not kinder-gardeners, not even 5-10 year Old. ALL AGES! Now I am going to inform you on a lot of puzzles you can buy at your local toy store or you can make your own store that sells nothing but puzzles!

Dear Puzzle makers of the world.

I have a few suggestions for new kinds of puzzles. A mystery irregular border, or a two-sided puzzle called Then and Now. Today's product on one side and yesterday's product on the other. Or maybe a game called Enigma. Comes with icosahedron* dice and instructions.. Puzzles not included. Puzzles made from a change sticker and POG ingredients. Or puzzles of kids magazine covers. For those of you that don't know. Change stickers change when you move them. Company logo link letters, Times Square and Las Vegas light up puzzles. Or puzzles made out of gak, silly putty, and newspaper. These are perfect materials for puzzles. I hope these are good ideas you can keep inside your head and use them when you need a little excitement in your life. If you feel preoccupied, and you need something to boost your boredom, you can come for some more ideas. Or you could make them up yourself. Either way, puzzles are a sure way to occupy your life in an exciting way.
In conclusion, if you want to shake the blues out of your life ... Grab a puzzle.

*An Icosahedron is a 20-sided geometric shape.

Nicholas was diagnosed with Asperger's at age 4. Mom says he has his own computer and writes for a little bit almost every day – stories, "emails" (which never get sent because his computer is not connected to the Internet), lists, and other bits and pieces of things. Almost everything Nicholas writes is make-believe and pertains to his perseverative interests – babies, elevators, apartment houses, and his imagined "grown-up family" (his wife, Catherine, and his kids, Steve and Samantha).

The spelling, grammar, and punctuation are exactly as Nicholas wrote them.

Cookie Girl

By Nicholas, at age 4

Once upon a time, there was a girl, whose name was Cookie Girl.
She loved to bake lots and lots and lots of cookies.
She had a store and a string of bells her friend, Mr. Bear, had given to her as a present for her kindness.
On a nice and sunny day, her oven suddenly broke down!
"Oh, no! What will I do?"
Then, Baby Bunny came into the store.
" What's wrong Cookie Girl?"
She told him and he said that his dad was a repairman and that he could come repair the oven.
Cookie Girl was so happy and relieved!
The man came and fixed the oven very quickly.
Cookie Girl told him he could come any time for a free cookie!
THE END

Samantha's Trip to Spain

By Nicholas, at age 5

Once upon a time, Samantha and her parents, Catherine and Nicholas went on a trip. Samantha had never been on an airplane before. She was very excited. Daddy was taking time off of work, a vacation, to make the trip. They boarded the airplane and it flew for a very long time. It took such a long time that Samantha ate 2 meals and watched one movie and even had a nap. When she woke up, they were there. They were in Spain. Samantha was very excited that they were in Spain so that she could practice speaking Spanish. She said "hola" to everyone as they walked by. She said "gracias" to the cab driver and waitresses. She said "como te llamas?" when she met a new Spanish friend, Linda, at the park. She even learned a few new words like "amigo" and "viaje." She said "Adios" when it was time to go home and leave Linda. When she got home, she was happy to see her old friends and tell them about her trip. She wrote emails and letters to Linda and they stayed friends forever. The End.

Steve

By Nicholas, at age 5-1/2

A new baby Steve. He is a very happy baby. He has blond hair and blue eyes. He weighs 10-78 lbs. When he Grows 90-100 lbs he will become a Teenager & a author. He really likes books and sports. His favorite book is "The Cat and the Hat." Why is he a boy 'cause that's what God decided. His favorite food is spinach. He knows it will help him grow up big and strong. Why he wants to be helthy 'Cause he wants to be 7 yrs old. His favorite color is green (like spinach!) That is funny. his other favorite color is pink.

One day Steve went for a ride on his bike. He decided to go to the park. His favorite ride at the park is the slide. He likes going down the big slide and yelling, "Hoorah!!!!" when Steve gets home Samantha gets on her tricycle & gets to the park her favorite ride is the swing.

Steve played W/ Nicholas Samantha had a fun time playing on the swing.

After ad Steve's favorite spinach and chicken. Steve ate all his food and got to pick out his dessert. When Samantha gets home she plays w/ her mommy for 10:00min. it's 9:52p time to go to sleep.

The end.

Starting Point

By Nicholas, at age 5

Nicholas, the dad he gently walks though the doors, Automatic
doors. The automatic door opened it for him. Mark, the di-
rector of the building, got 3-three pieces of paper,
1-one **black** ink stamp to write the word of the book for him,
2-two bags of **gray** staples, and one **black** and gray stapleler.
Then someone said- Mark: "Here's your card" It was Mark
Then someone else said- Nicholas the dad: "Thank you!"
said Nicholas. "You have to go on level 2. This is level *L.
Okay!" Just Follow these Dierctions, And Don't take the
stairs.
(Nicholas pushing the elevator button)
"Doors opening" Story Narrator: Baby boy, Baby joe and Baby
Girl, Baby Samantha
Thought it was intersting that a elevator could ever talk!
"Welcome to this elevator! Please Do Not lean On Doors. Never
Leave Your child
underseated because you could get hurt,... ...and your child will
be stuck in this elevator or it will never come out. Thank
you going up from *L to level 2.
Up, up, up. Level 2. Please Do Not lean On Doors. Doors
Closeing."
Nicholas, counting from 200-208: 200, 201, 202, 203 204, 205, 206,
207, 2 ... 2 ... 208!
The End!

Baby's Imagination

By Nicholas, at age 5

Chapter 1 – Every Night Baby Slept

One night the baby decided she was not very tired. So she got out of her crib and decided to go for a long walk. But baby's don't walk! But she was using her imagination, so she began to walk. But this was too slow, so she decided to start running. But baby's don't run! But she was using her imagination. Baby thought she wasn't going fast enough so she decided to start flying! But baby's don't fly!!! But she was using her imagination, so she started to fly. She flew right out of the house and up in the sky. She decided to go back in her house after the ride. She got to stay up until 8:52.

Chapter 2 – Breakfast Was

Then she flew over to gramma's house. and said "Gramma do you have any breakfast?" "Eggs, toast,
Bacon, pancakes, Milkshake with chocolate." replied gramma. Then baby ate and ate the big breakfast that gramma made delicious! and said "Mmmmmmmmmmmmmmmmmmmmm" "Yummy" she said.

Forrest's Favorite Food (and toy, and president)

"I like hammers because they start with 'ham'!"

– Forrest, at age 3

"Do you know who my favorite president is?
Abraham Lincoln because his name has 'ham' in it."

– Forrest, at age 4

Commercially Minded

Forrest, at age 5

"Did you know that Home Depot was a proud sponsor of the Olympics?"

The Lord's Prayer – Breanna's Version

By Breanna, at age 2

Our father, who art in heaven, hallowed be thy name.
Thy kingdom come, thy will be done, on earth as it is in heaven.
Give us this day, our GARLIC BREAD,
and forgive us our trespasses, as we forgive those who trespass
   against us.
And lead us not into temptation, but deliver us from evil,
For thine is the kingdom, and the power, and the glory,
Forever and ever, Amen.

Mom says Garlic bread has always been Breanna's favorite food.

The students in David's third-grade class had to each make a time-line of the most significant events in their lifetime.

My Personal Timeline

By David, at age 8

1995   Born, May 7

1996   1 year old, May 7

1998   Pre school

2000   Kindergarten

            First trip to Disney World

2001   1st grade

            Get Nintendo 64

2002   Get PS2*

2003   Start 3rd grade

Present   Made this timeline

*That's Playstation 2, for you video game novices.

D Is for Khalid

By Khalid, at age 9

D is for Khalid. Why?
Because Khalid likes dinosaurs and dogs.
He is the one who loves paleontology.
He is afraid of the dark.
He hates shots.
He is proud of my baby brother Cayden.
He wishes to travel around the world.
He will someday be a paleontologist.
D is for Khalid. Why?
Because Khalid likes dinosaurs and dogs.

By Andrew

I Wish I Were Not So Obsessed

By David, at age 11

I wish I were not so obsessed.
I know everything about every show I've ever watched.
Give me a question about a comic story,
I can get it.
My brain exists in the Internet more than in real life.
My eyes see more of video games than real life.
While most kids wait for the next physical game, I wait for the
     next video game.
Rather than having my room filled with pictures of sports stars,
It has pictures of the stars of comics.
Outside games are usually a myth to me.
Movie fanatic? You bet.
If someone were to cut open my head and read my mind, they
     would lose theirs,
It would blow up from being stuffed with such useless junk.
Not that I hate having it.

By Russell

A Unique Perspective

I"f a man does not keep pace with his companions, perhaps it is because he hears a different drummer."

– Henry David Thoreau

People with Asperger Syndrome often think differently than the rest of us. Literally. Scientists have shown that the neural pathways in people with Asperger's have actually formed differently from those in neurotypicals' brains.

It can be tough to be "different." But it takes people who are "different" to create breathtaking works of art, or devise brilliant new theories in science – or even make us howl with laughter as they make us see the world from a different perspective.

Not every child with Asperger Syndrome will grow up to be an Einstein or a Mozart. But every single one can teach us something new, something different ... something valuable.

By Zak

Rocks

By Josh, at age 9

Do rocks love to roll and tumble?
Do they ever worry if they crumble?
Are they jealous of the heads on Mt. Rushmore?
Does erosion ever make them sore?

While it's true that children with Asperger Syndrome typically have trouble understanding sarcasm, many LEARN to recognize it. And quite a few of our kiddos enjoy practicing it themselves.

Aspie Sarcasm

By Forrest, at age 4

Dad: "What part of 'quiet' don't you understand?"

Forrest: **"E T."**

Tim's second-grade teacher was very unhappy with Tim's report on the class field trip to Boston, arguing that he had noticed all the wrong things. But Tim wasn't interested in Boston – he was interested in Warrenville, CT, for which he'd memorized the map and all the school bus routes.

Field Trip Report
(by a Future Pulitzer Prize winner*)

By Tim Page, in second grade

Well, we went to Boston, Massachusetts through the town of Warrenville, Connecticut on Route 44A. It was very pretty and there was a church that reminded me of pictures of Russia from our book that is published by Time-Life. We arrived in Boston at 9:17. At 11 we went on a big tour of Boston on Gray Line 43, made by the Superior Bus Company like School Bus Six, which goes down Hunting Lodge Road where Maria lives and then on to Separatist Road and then to South Eagleville before it comes to our school. We saw lots of good things like the Boston Massacre site. The tour ended at 1:05. Before I knew it we were going home. We went through Warrenville again but it was too dark to see much. A few days later it was Easter. We got a cuckoo clock.*

*Bus routes and maps weren't Tim's only interests, though, as he explained in his 2007 New Yorker *article "Parallel Play, A Lifetime of Restless Isolation Explained": His "first and most powerful obsession was music – the same records played again and again while I watched them spin, astonished at their evocation of aural worlds that I not only instinctively understood even as a toddler but in which I actually felt comfortable." Tim turned*

that obsession and ability into a career as a music critic, first for the SoHo News, *then the* New York Times, Newsday, *and* The Washington Post. *In 1997, he was awarded the Pulitzer Prize for music criticism, for "his lucid and illuminating music criticism." It was not until three years later, at age 46, that Tim was diagnosed with Asperger Syndrome.*

* From "Parallel Play, A lifetime of restless isolation explained" by T. Page, August 20, 2007, *The New Yorker*. Copyright 2007 by Tim Page. Adapted with permission.

A Child Who Values Authenticity

Nick, at age 4

"I'm getting tired of my little rubber bat. I want a real vampire bat with rabies."

The Six Stages of Not Getting Something You Really Want

David, at age 9

After 8 of the 12 kids in David's (Asperger's/high-functioning autism) classroom had made honor roll, and one of the four who didn't had a meltdown.

David: "I've now figured out The Six Stages of Not Getting Something You Really Want:

1) Sadness

2) Denial

3) Beginning of Acceptance

4) Temporary Insanity. Like running up to people and saying things like 'Smell my breath' and 'Ooh, do you know that panda bears have a really weird way of mating?'

5) Anger

Repeat Steps 3-4 a couple times, until you finally reach the final stage ...

6) MAJOR ANGER!!!"

Mom: (A little baffled, wondering where her fourth grader had ever heard Elisabeth Kubler-Ross' five stages of grief.) "What about 'Acceptance?' Don't you ever get to Acceptance?"

David: "Maybe. I'm not sure. The bus came."

I Am Like a Cat

By Samuel, at age 14

I am like a cat that sometimes needs time alone.
I am like a cat that sometimes loves to be around others.
I like routine and don't like changes.

I am like a cat because sometimes I ignore everything.
I am like a cat because sometimes I really pay attention.
I'm a finicky eater, but I love bird meat.

I am like a cat that is intelligent.
I am like a cat; I usually land on my feet.
I'm usually gentle, but throw a hissy fit now and then.

I am like a cat.

What Kind of Cat?

Jonah R, at age 5

"Is our cat a cartoon cat or a live action cat?"

A Heavenly Pet

Forrest, at age 4

"I know why it rains. It rains because God's dog drools."

Beating Wings

By Claire, at age 17

All
I can
Do is stand
And watch and hear
The beating of wings
That had once been so white,
For I know now that
My dove is gone,
And I walk
With no
One.

Broken Clouds

Aidan, at age 3

When Aidan was 3 years old, he commented on a beautiful Arizona sunset while hiking. It was one of his first multiple-word utterances.

Aidan: "Clouds are broken. Sun crash through them."

Dreams ...

By Zak, at age 10

... so delicate like leaves hovering over a still pond, floating on the silky surface ...
... the moon ...
... just like the imagination, glowing with intelligence and curiosity ...
... you can choose your future ...
... one path at a time.

Colin is 8 years old and has high-functioning autism. He wrote the following story in a single paragraph, but we've broken it into several to make it easier to follow. (By the way, Mom tells us his middle name is not really Oxide – he changed it to that on his own.)

The Two Sheeps Gruff

By Colin "Oxide" R, at age 8

Once upon a time, there were two Sheeps Gruff. Two of those Sheeps name was smallest and biggest for size. There was a troll who lived under the stairs. The two Sheeps Gruff are so hungry. Today is Friday and they want to go to McDonalds. They are going on the Happy Meal Adventure.

First, the Sheeps will go down to the stairs and watch out for the troll. Next, they jump over the mountains and go to the McDonalds restaurant.

First, the small Sheep is going down the steps. STOMP ... STOMP ... STOMP ... The first Sheep stomps down the stairs.

Suddenly, the troll jumps out and says, "Who's stomping all over my stairs?!" The Sheep answered, "I'm the first Sheep Gruff and I am going to McDonalds to eat, eat, eat, and get fat and grow up."

The troll said, "No, No, No, You're Not! Now I'll gobble you up!" The small Sheep said, "No, no, no. Don't eat me. I'll go to the mountain, and the second sheep Gruff is really big. He will come. Let me pass."

The troll said, "Ohhhh ... so now go."

Now the last Sheep Gruff goes down the stairs. STOMP ... STOMP ... STOMP... STAMP ... STAMP ... STAMP ... BING ... BONG ... BING ... BANG ... BANG ... BANG ...

So, the Sheep Gruff was too heavy. Now the stairs start to crack. "Who's cracking the stairs?!! You're making me ANGRY!" said the troll.

"I'm the second Sheep Gruff. I am making it fat and grow up and change the number," said the second Sheep. The voice was louder than the troll.

"Oh yeah! Now I'll gobble you up. You have snow and hooves and a tail and this sheep belongs to Bo Peep," said the troll.

"I'll show them. I'll throw you into the river," said the Sheep.

Now the second Sheep Gruff is charging after the troll and head butted the troll. The troll fell down and went into the river, and the fish ate it.

The two Sheeps Gruff jumped over the mountain and made it to the McDonalds restaurant. The stairs cracked and broke into pieces. The two Sheeps Gruff got fat and changed the number from age 24 to age 25 and grew up. Their tails grew longer and longer and longer. They lived happily ever after. The End.

The Problem With Dreams

Jonah, at age 5

"I don't like to have dreams. When you dream you can't think about anything except what you're dreaming."

Age of Wisdom

Jonah, at age 5

"After people turn 98, they turn 99. After people turn 99, they turn into letters. First they're A, then they're B, then they're C ... all the way to Z. And after they turn into letters, they turn into planets. Then they die."

If I Were in Charge of the World

By Henry, at age 14

If I were in charge of the world,
I'd cancel pollution,
Monday mornings,
Clothes as presents for Christmas and also
Terrorists.

If I were in charge of the world,
There'd be strict environmental regulations,
Cats, dogs, and most invasive animals would be removed from
New Zealand, and
A device that downloaded information directly into the brain.

If I were in charge of the world,
You wouldn't have claustrophobia.
You wouldn't have homework.
You wouldn't have bad neighborhoods.
Or, "Just one more math problem" (followed by about three more)!

If I were in charge of the world,
Mom's cookies would be a vegetable.
All science fiction movies would be rated G.
And a person who sometimes forgot how to solve a math problem,
And sometimes forgot to bring their lunch box,
Would still be allowed to be
In charge of the world.

Insanity: What Is It?

By David, at age 12

Much to your surprise, you're probably insane. No, it isn't that only psychos read this (In fact, they wouldn't read it, because they would spend too much time complaining about the voices in their heads telling them to do things). It is because I believe most people are insane. I think of insanity as a filter. As you perceive something, that filter throws into the mix emotions, irrationality, and some other factors. This causes you to perceive something other then exactly what it is, changed to fit you and your perceptions. Other filters include different preferences, Autism/Asperger's (in the form of sensory input being affected), and others. The "Insanity Filter" (I'll call it I.F.) affects it on the most fundamental level, with your perceptions altering what you see, hear and feel.

This brings up another question. What about the people we consider insane? Are they the "sane" ones? I don't think so. If they were sane, they would all be perceiving the same thing (unless we're crazier then I think, and our perceptions are so filtered that we don't really know anything about the universe), unless I am interpreting sanity incorrectly. This means they are probably just crazier then most of us, as in their perceptions are so filtered that they don't get even an approximation of reality in one or more areas. Basically, their I.F. is too strong, or isn't working right. So, that brings up the question… what *is* sane anyway? Someone with no I.F. What would they be like? I think there are three possibilities.

1. They would be completely logical, with irrationality, emotion and other common filters not coming into the equation at all, insofar as perceptions of reality. Also, they would all be perceiving the exact same thing.

2. There are no sane people. Our filters are stronger then we think, and we get no real approximation of reality, although our filters are very similar. True reality is so complex that if we were exposed to it, our brains would shut down.

3. Reality is almost as complex as in theory #2, but the few who have no filters can perceive it correctly. They almost certainly are among who we consider insane, while maybe all the others are in hiding somewhere.

Even if I am wrong in every way, I still probably got you to think about things in a different way. If I'm right, maybe I'll prove it someday. Or maybe someone will read this and be inspired, and go on to prove it themselves. If the last one is right, then whoever proves it has my blessing.

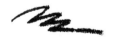

Joseph wrote this poem in seventh grade after a family trip to the beach. He spent a large part of the day digging a hole and then filling it with water. Experts might call this "perseverative behavior" in a 12-year-old child on the spectrum. But without this poem, would they recognize the complex thought processes that were at work?

Diffusion

By Joseph, at age 12

I dig a hole in the sand.
It's much easier than on land.
I'll fill the hole to the top.
Fill with seawater, I must not stop.
No matter how many buckets I use,
I find the water will just diffuse.
Into the surrounding sand it seeps.
It's almost enough to make me weep.
I suddenly realize what it must be.
The water seeps to the level of the sea.
I'm no longer sad with my new conclusion.
I just learned a lesson about diffusion.

Travel can be very trying for children on the spectrum (and their families!). Many of our kiddos get great comfort from familiar surroundings and circumstances. Travel can mean new places, new faces, and even new foods, and that means lots of stress! Anna, who has high-functioning autism, wrote the following piece in her personal journal. Mom says Anna did NOT want to take this trip, but she did an impressive job of expressing her feelings, rather than melting down.

Family Trip

By Anna C, at age 11

I'm writing a topic now on TRAVEL. In October we took a trip to Cooperstown, NY, because Mom heard that the town was nice. The town in fact was NICE! It's just small streets that lead to a back quiet street with houses, and looks down on to Lake Otsego Park. In the back way of the street are cars parked along and just quiet houses, and backs of shops, and the streets lead down one quiet street to one other with houses, and parked cars. But parking in town was hard.

The Pennsylvania countryside roads were beautiful. It was another part of Pennsylvania that goes to New York. When we usually travel, we drive through New Jersey, Connecticut, New York, Massachusetts and New Hampshire. Mostly for autumn, summer and spring vacation, we go to Popham Beach, Maine. We usually vacation to Maine, our old hometown. What wasn't good about Maine was there wasn't a lot of stuff, we didn't know that many people, and worst of all we were far away from our grandparents. But they came to Popham with us in the spring (in May), and in the summer (in June), my birthday month, and we saw them for the holiday (Christmas) season. But what I DID like about Maine was that we had a nice big yard, it was quieter up there, and we could throw our ball soooo high! I like that there is more stuff down here, and we're so close to our grandparents.

It was a wonderful drive to New York. It was a NEW part of Pennsylvania we drove through and the country was nice. We had several towns to drive through, before we got to Cooperstown. When you're really close you see little drives and houses and farms and roads. When you first come in, it's a wonderful town. And best of all, it's everything baseball, and there's a nice Baseball Hall of Fame. When we finally parked we got some lunch from a cafe and I ate my own food down by Lake Otsego. After lunch, Daddy called his brother, and he was in the Hall of Fame with his family.

We went to the museum and met Daddy's brother, his wife, and our six-year-old and little baby cousin. We love them. Lena read on her favorite baseball players, and we watched a baseball game in the theater. And in the shop Lena got a t-shirt, and a Hall of Fame mug. I was bored, ready to go, and not as interested in baseball as much as Lena was.

But even on that, I held up okay. I was thirsty and needed to get straight to the motel. The only thing I wanted to do, not have any water (I did that), not get to our motel (I did that). The only thing I needed to do was get back home the next day! To my familiar house!

And our relatives stayed next door to our room! As soon as we got to our motel, The Lakeview, that had a nice view of the lake, we checked in. After that, I ran to get some water and then we went outside, where Lena and our 6-year-old cousin ran around. I played a little with them, but mostly I just relaxed outside. But then me, Daddy, Daddy's brother, Lena, Aaron (my six-year-old cousin) and me drove into town, went into stores that evening, ordered take-out for dinner (not for me).

Daddy brought a homemade cake for dessert also. We ate dinner, and I ate one of my foods. Before, our cousin said (he didn't know it was our kind of cake) he wanted soooooo much cake. And in the end, he didn't like it.

We all slept well, even I did, even though I missed my room at home and it was a new place, I slept well.

The next morning, Lena went to meet our relatives in their room. Even though I didn't want her to leave, I came with her. We were going to have cake for breakfast with them, but we didn't.

After that, we drove into town, looked back in the Hall of Fame, and looked in the sports memorabilia shops and bought Lena a Red Sox license plate. After that we went into a deli and ordered a little lunch for the rest of the family. Then we went for coffee at a shop, down a back street. And we had a picnic at Lake Otsego where our cousins and me and Lena played. It was soooooo crowded there because of a Pumpkin Festival.

After lunch we said goodbye to Daddy's family and our cousins, and climbed in the car and headed back home. It was a nice drive through New York. I was so anxious to be home. When we got to Pennsylvania, I kept asking, "Are we there yet? Are we there yet?" I felt homesick in Cooperstown and wanted to cry the whole way home.

At last, things began to look familiar: The New Jersey turnpike, the tollbooth, the inn we pass every time we go out. Our street, our yard, our house. We finally made it to our house. The first thing I did when we arrived back home, while the rest of the family unpacked and watched the football game, was write on the computer. That night, I felt safe again, and glad to be home, eating dinner in my familiar dining room, my favorite dinner. And then cake for dessert. Then I was too tired to hang out, so I ran straight up to bed. It felt good to be finally home in my own room, sleeping in my familiar bed. Sound and safe, in a familiar place.

David's parents worried that their 3-year-old son, who so hated any kind of change, would have a rough time on his first vacation (to an ocean-side resort in Maine). But after they told him the plan, he repeated this mantra for the entire week leading up to the trip.

David WAS excited about his upcoming vacation, but there was a bit of a misunderstanding. Fortunately, he figured out his own way to deal with it.

Vacation Plans

David, at age 3

"We'll get in Mommy's blue car [license plate] BCX-421,
go to the airport,
get in the airplane,
go to Ma-Mane,
get a jeep,
go to vacation,
and then play Blue's Clues."

The whole trip, including 90 minutes on a plane and several hours in a car, went smoothly. Until, that is, the family arrived at their cabin:

"Where's the TV? No TV? I WANNA GO HOME!"

Apparently "playing Blues Clues" didn't mean playing with his stuffed Blue doggy and other Blues Clues toys, but playing the video tape he had at home. But after an initial meltdown, David came up with his own way of dealing with the stress. For the rest of the trip, he sang over and over (albeit in manic double-time):

"We are going to play Blue's Clues
We are going to play Blue's Clues
We are going to play Blue's Clue
Because we're really smart!"

During an end-of-the-year school program in which the teacher was recognizing students for reading achievement, a classmate received 100 Accelerated Reading Points – quite an accomplishment.

A Logical Argument

Tyler, at age 7

Tyler: "I only got 20 points."

Mom: "How did the other student receive so many?"

Tyler: "She read a lot of books."

Mom: "Well, you read a lot of books."

Tyler: "Yeah, but she took the tests."

Mom: "Well, do you know how to take the tests?"

Tyler: "Yeah."

Mom: "Well, why didn't you take the tests then?"

Tyler: "You know, Mom, there's more to life than taking tests."

Abigail says this poem is not about having Asperger's. It's about someone who can fly.

Find the World

By Abigail, at age 11

If there is something Different about me
That I do not show, you will find a thing
And then you will know.
You will know.

Find the little thing,
a compliment of spring,
find the little thing as you know it,

Find the little thing
a compliment of spring,
find the little thing as you show it.

See how the stars shoot by!
In the bright (dark) sky!
See the stars shoot by!
I feel we all can fly!

Wouldn't that be nice
With a bit of spice
Bit of fairy spice
That will let you fly.

([*Fairy*] Dust is another word
But certainly not *turd*).
Someone wants for me
To fly and be me

Flying over the Mountainous State,
Oh how I feel that it couldn't be better
I have been working on the perfect remedy
for people's wishes: Dearly love to fly.

Oh, Wingz, teach me your group song,
And I'll join your club with wings.

I'll fly over rainbows, and skies of rain
To deliver what has not yet been delivered to its rightful place,
Oh so sweetly; it could not be that I love the unwinged race.

Some may call me a racist, but no one bothers me.
They regard me as a freak of nature and will not play with me
no matter how many times I ask them; oh how lonely I do feel.

Wingz club hear me shouting from alaska to brazil.
Hear me now, I have so much to relate but just listen,
I have wings.

What If?

By David, at age 11

A lot of the things I worry about in life are,
What if bugs crawl on me?
What if I get beat up at school?
What if lots of people hate me?
What if I get hit by lightning?
What if I lose at everything?
What if nobody helps me?
What if I lose all my friends?
What if I don't do well in school?
What if I don't do well in life?
What if I get in trouble?
What if I lose my pets?
What if nobody likes me?

Sometimes when I am feeling fine, the what-ifs come and
shake me up.

By Rilind

By Andrew

Growing up on the Spectrum

"*Life is not easy for any of us. But what of that? We must have perseverance and above all confidence in ourselves. We must believe that we are gifted for something, and that this thing, at whatever cost, must be attained.*"

— Marie Curie

Growing up is hard. As adults, we tend to reminisce about the freedom, the fun, and the lazy summer days we had as children. But for most of us, all that fun was interspersed with a heaping helping of insecurities, anxieties, and – during the teen years – pure angst.

For many children with Asperger Syndrome, those growing pains are multiplied 10-fold – if not 50-fold! Imagine having to navigate school, especially middle school, without being able to read facial expressions, recognize sarcasm, or grasp unspoken rules. Add to that being clumsy and maybe having some odd habits. It's the perfect recipe for becoming the victim or the social outcast.

Yet, this section isn't all sad. While there are some heart-wrenching tales, there are also some happy endings. As I read what these kids wrote, I was struck by the difference that one person – one friend or teacher, one person who "gets" them and accepts them as they are – can make.

The Way It Is

Khalid, at age 9

"Sometimes I get mad easily and then I know that the other kids are looking at me and calling me a freak in their heads, so basically it's just really weird having Asperger Syndrome."

Escape Plan

Jonah, at age 5

"I want to find a door out of Planet Earth."

Heartbreak

Brennan, at age 5

After a very frustrating morning, Brennan finally dissolved into a sobbing jag that would break your heart. Mom suggested that maybe they should try praying.

Brennan: "No Mom, God doesn't care. He just lets you cry."

The World's a Stage

Jonah, at age 5

"I am always in a movie, and I am always quoting from the movie that I am in."

I Can't Stop Thinking of Home

By David, at age 11

I can't stop thinking of home,
Where I can do the things I like.
Where I can play with my friends,
I can play with my games,
And I can do what I like.
Where comics and fun abound.
Where I can sleep at night with my dogs and my cats,
after a day of school and work,
And where I can look to my own little world,
And see how it will be tomorrow.

The Lamb

By Randy, at age 17

He walks into school each day with his head held low
Wondering why life is so bad
He walks down the hall and into class
Knowing that there is misery to be had

The way to lunch is like walking a plank
Over a dark, stormy sea
With nowhere to run or hide
But still longing to be free

He sees the rest of his peers
Having the time of their lives
While he sits in the corner
Alone and full of spite

Deep down he envies them
Because their egos are so tall
Little does he know that without him
They wouldn't feel that way at all

For he is the lamb
The sacrifice that has been made
To elevate the students elite
Above their shallow restraints

If there were no lamb there wouldn't be
Someone from the top to look down upon
And add to the belief
That they are the biggest fish in the sea

Sometimes he thinks of revenge
And how sweet it would be
Only to realize its futility
And its sheer stupidity

All he really wants, however
Is to be treated with respect
And not with the cruel hate
That plagues the entire sect

As the lamb lies in bed
And begins to rest his head
He begins to hate his life
And he dreads the day to start again

Patterns

By David, at age 12

When Mom tells David "No more grapes" and he replies "Just three more!," he has a good reason — he has to finish his chewing pattern. While children with obsessive compulsive disorder might perform patterned behavior because of obsessions or fears, lots of children on the autism spectrum just enjoy them. Or, as David has explained, because they just feel "right."

Left=L ; Right=R

I think about patterns in my head all the time. For example, I could think LRRL. But then I would go further. Like LRRL RLLR RLLR LRRL. And then I could go even further, like adding RLLR LRRL LRRL RLLR, then doing the second one again, then doing the first one again, to keep everything even. I even have patterns for eating, walking ... a lot of stuff.

For example, with bite-sized food, I take two pieces and chew on them hard on the left side of my mouth, then two hard for the right side, then I take one piece and chew it softly in the right side of my mouth, then one soft for the left. I repeat it four times, and for which hands I use to pick them up, it's the first pattern I wrote, LRRL RLLR RLLR LRRL. Then I repeat. I bet it's starting to seem complicated, huh? Well, for me, they're not. In fact, they're almost like second nature. I could tell you many more patterns, but then again, the book isn't quite big enough.

Lots of people would just say, "Oh man, that must be crazy, I'd go nuts in a day, how do you bear it?" Well, the truth is, it's pretty easy. Once I think up a pattern, it's in my head, and I know it by heart. It might seem crazy to you. Well you know what I think? I think you're absolutely right. But I like it.

By Colin

I'm Okay

Kevin, at age 7

After Kevin was diagnosed with Asperger Syndrome at age 7, his mom planned carefully how to explain the diagnosis to him. She wanted to be sure he'd understand that even though he might be "different" from other kids, he was still okay. She was determined to help him have a positive self-image, but still worried that he might be confused and possibly angry or depressed.

Finally, Mom started the discussion one day when they were playing outside in the yard.

Mom: "Hey, Kev, you've heard of 'Asperger Syndrome,' right?"

Kevin: "Yeah, but I still just don't get what it is."

So Mom tried to describe some of the idiosyncrasies of Asperger's, and asked Kevin if he noticed that other kids at school didn't seem to do or say some of those same types of things.

Kevin: "No, I don't know what you're talking about!"

Mom: "Kevin, when you're around the other kids at school, do you ever feel like you're a little different than them?"

Kevin: "No. I feel like I'm okay. But they're all a little weird."

172

What One Autistic Feels All the Time

By Danielle, at age 16

I have always felt of autism as a new species of humans. We don't have any physical differences, yet our minds are over or under advanced than the present human race.

I have always seen the world different than others. Everyone sees a movie with interest to watch it, but I see them as something to study. People talk to each for enjoyment. I just talk to get an ice cream cone. I feel those without autism have no purpose for talking to people. I just do it to live out my life.

I've studied other autistics up close (forgive the adjective) and I've noticed that there are certain groups within the actual high-functioning autism/Asperger Syndrome category. There are those that copy lines from movies incessantly, typically boys, and there are those that are tortuously quiet, mostly girls.

There are even those that have assimilated so closely into the "'typical" kids' world that no one sees any difference. I like testing this out. When I meet a new person that wants to be friends with me I pretended I was typical and even said those typical, boring lines. "Hi. How are you? Great. How are you?"

If I can get past the "how are you" thing, I'm usual there. Then we hang out, and by the end of the year they left me or I them. Friends just don't seem to interest me as much as others. They're such as job: I have to call them once a week, I have to act interested in things that bore me, and to top that it's impossible to end the friendship without hurting the person. To solve this problem I end friendships before they start. No matter how much I like someone I don't talk to them.

It's kind of ironic with my views on dating. I never date boys, even if I suddenly liked them. To me, all people that date eventually dump the person. There's rarely a case where their first date comes through and they date until marriage. I don't even have time for that. I'm too busy, which makes things even more annoying.

This rambling isn't going to help much, is it? This cursed autistic brain causes me to change subject every two seconds unless I control it. I'm just letting it go free so people get see what one autistic feels all the time.

My Life

By Randy, at age 17

Life at times can seem very purposeless, as if we are rats trapped in a maze blindly running after a piece of cheese that is constantly being moved or manipulated by the uncaring and unsympathetic researcher. We are often unaware that a world exists outside the maze that is so much larger and contains such greater ideas and opportunities than our petty struggle for the cheese that we can hardly fathom it. Yet we are so engrossed by our hopeless struggle for the fleeting satisfaction of the cheese that we never look up. That conflict has been the primary catalyst in my admittedly short life.

For my entire life I have lived in a small typical American town that many wouldn't see as anything special. I've always had mixed feelings about it. I liked how it was anonymously tucked into a little corner away from pretty much anything special. Because of that it always provided a sense of hollow, but still comforting security. However, I never felt the connection to the town that most people feel towards their hometowns. I always kind of saw it as just there, like a background in a grandiose painting that is obscured by shadow. Besides, I've always enjoyed staying home in my own little space more than going out into the unbridled chaos that is the world.

My earliest memories were just of me staying at home with my mother, who had left her job as a hospital RN to care for me. She preferred it to working anyway. Most of my memories were vague and spotty at best, but my mother always devoted her full attention to me. My father was hardly ever home, and when he was, he was usually sleeping. He did teach me how to read and do basic arithmetic before I entered preschool, which gave me a considerable advantage, albeit dooming me to mind-numbing boredom during my first few years of school. That spurred my life long love of reading and I have been doing it ever since I could decipher a few of the words. My father was extremely perplexing to my young mind. He was both extremely happy and jolly or in a barbaric rage. Nonetheless, I lived a generally happy and carefree life before I entered school.

Being dropped off in preschool was like being dropped off in purgatory, for the only thing that was keeping me going was the thought that at some point my mother would walk through the door and save me. Aside from being bored to death by a droning teacher who constantly repeated things I already knew, I also had an extremely difficult time both re-lating to and getting along with other children. I lived in my own little world that was light years away from where they were. Those aliens were both frightened yet oddly intrigued by me. They sensed my weakness like a dog and exploited it constantly. What could I do? There was just one physically and socially weak me against all of them. My only option was to withdraw even further and live purely in myself. It was at that moment that my distrust of the human race truly began.

Kindergarten was more of the same, only worse because it was longer and my mom had started working again. The kids were just as vicious, and I was still alone and detached. Then in first grade there was a major change. I was assigned an aide by the name of Mrs. Fox. She was like a second mother to me. Her compassion and concern was definitely helpful, yet her presence made me feel even more abnormal and alienated. In a way, she became my only source of in-school interaction.

Recess was the worst. I used to sit under a tree that was far removed from the incomprehensible joy of the others. I simply sank into my mind to relive the emptiness.

Second grade started out as more of the same. I still felt as if I was a freak of nature and that I did not fit into the school mosaic. I was still very secluded, and when others were either playing or socializing, I sat in a corner and read. At this point I still seldom spoke, not even to Mrs. Fox. Then one day there was a shift. A girl whose name I will not mention, purely out of respect, actually noticed me. I didn't know what to make of it, for the crushing loneliness had grown so prevalent that I had almost gone numb to it. Yet I was elated. Someone noticed me, someone cared enough to break through, someone liked me and was interested in me. Of course I had my parents, but anyone will tell you that it is simply not the same as having someone your age, someone who had child thoughts and concerns unlike the mammoth colossal maddening burdens of adulthood. It also probably didn't hurt that I thought that she was the prettiest thing that I had ever laid eyes on. Someone had turned the dimmer switch up a few notches.

I have not mentioned home in a while, simply because it was a constant. I was always glad to be there, for it was my sanctuary from the storm that was constantly brewing outside. When I was home I loved to just go to my room and read. I loved it because they took you away to a world that is usually much more interesting than our own. At times I felt like I knew the characters like best friends including the villains. I liked movies and TV, but I preferred books because they required total immersion to be enjoyed. A highlight of the time was when my grandparents took me to Disney World, which I enjoyed. I think what I was really feeling was the joy of being with them. All they did was constantly spoil me! I really can't remember much about my elementary school home life except for the fact that my inner geek was beginning to show through my growing Star Wars collection.

As middle school began to roll around, some things started to change. I was beginning to express my anxiety and frustration with myself. Things really took a dive when I hit seventh grade. There I was angry, anxious, paranoid and depressed. When these emotions are combined, it becomes like an old abandoned and long neglected building, for eventually it will implode and collapse. Although I received excellent grades, I was constantly bogged down by discipline problems. Now that I reflect back on it, another reason why I think that I may have had such problems was simply because I was bored. I breezed through every single class and hardly ever socialized, so perhaps I was simply trying to shake things up. Regardless, there is no going back now.

I thought that things could not get any worse after seventh grade. I was dead wrong. All of the old problems from seventh grade persisted and new ones arose. Algebra 1 rolled around and for the first time I found myself struggling and I did not take it well. Sometimes just seeing math would cause my stomach to churn and just seeing it caused panic attacks. My life felt like a constant switch between anger and panic, never setting down in the middle. I felt like I was in a plane that was going down without a parachute. There was nothing I could do besides sit back and wait for it to crash. Outside of school, things weren't much better and I took out my anger and angst in all sorts of ways, which I now regret.

There were some bright spots though. Mrs. Fox was still firmly behind me, although I am at a loss at how she did it. My family tried everything they could, yet I felt sorry for them. The frustration with wanting to help but being unable to help me was crushing. I also found two things out about myself. For one, I could write. All of my papers and stories for both History and English were met with great praise. I thought nothing of it when I composed them, for I was simply emulating what I had from the multitudes of books that I had read. That gave me a much-needed boast, for I could create rather than destroy and vent my feelings through words other than through hurtful actions. I had made some friends as well who pretty much formed a breakfast club, for we so often got slammed with detention. We were all intelligent though and we were all video game nerds. Most importantly, however, my feelings for the girl had started to deepen. We started getting together and before I could get a finger on it I had my first girlfriend. This gave another reason not to hate myself, for another person depended on me as much as I depended on her.

My relationship with my father was always a roller coaster. He could go from fun and jolly into a raging inferno in seconds. Around this time, he retired and for graduating from eighth grade we went on a cross-country road trip. It was one of the greatest experiences in my life. The size, scope and sheer diversity of the country cannot be appreciated. However, the real reason was that my father and me connected in unimaginable ways, and our relationship has been strong ever since. It is amazing how just spending time with a person can connect you to him.

The transition to high school was tough, as is any transition, especially because two of my three old eighth grade friends left. However, a friend of mine from the neighborhood came in, so that eased it. I was still angry and disillusioned because I thought that high school would diminish these problems. However, I loved the more challenging workload that honors classes presented. I was in marching band, which was more chaos and panic than fun.

Then, towards the end of ninth grade, things started to change. Perhaps it was acceptance or maturity, but I think that I finally gazed up and realized the world outside the maze. I then committed myself to a goal that to many seemed preposterous: to be independent of Mrs. Fox by 11th grade. Their doubts actually further spurred me to prove them wrong and finally get the last laugh. I did it. The road was rough, but whenever there was a problem I simply fixed my flat and drove on into the unknown horizon.

When my 10th year was finally over, it was decided that I would indeed be liberated. We went out to dinner with Mrs. Fox and it was surprisingly somber to leave her. Tears were actually shed, although I knew that I should be happy. It is difficult to let go of an individual who has constantly stood by you when others thought you were hopeless.

When I looked up I felt as if I was reborn, as if the slate had gone blank, as if I had been granted a new understanding. I feel boundless and that if anyone attempts to chain me down, that I have the strength to emancipate myself. I am still not quite sure of what I want to do with my life, but I know that I will succeed, for I am capable of nothing short of what I aspire to be. If I can overcome this, there shall be no wall too high, no river too deep, no desert too vast and no wind too strong to hold me back. My future is limitless. I am free.

My Story of Survival

By Casey, at age 16

One of my earliest memories consists of me watching the other children run and play on the playground, making friends and socializing, while I sit on a bench a distance away, watching them and flapping my hands. I wanted so badly to be a part of their world, yet not so sure I wanted to be a part of it. It is the second week of kindergarten, and I am already considered an outsider.

Looking back on my childhood, I would say that I was very unhappy and stressed-out, no matter what *anybody* says. It wasn't until I was 8 years old, though, that I started to get depressed.

When I first started kindergarten, I barely talked and when I *did* talk you could barely understand me. Also, I did things such as flapping my hands, waving around ribbons or strings of grass, pacing, and muttering to myself. I guess the other kids noticed this and either avoided me or made fun of me. I had to repeat kindergarten, not because I was stupid, but because I had problems talking and getting along with the other kids. I took speech therapy and soon I was talking at what was expected for my age. When I was six years old I was diagnosed with high-functioning autism and ADHD. I did not find out about this until I was 12.

Throughout my elementary years, 50% of the kids avoided me, and the other half bullied me. They would do things like spit on me, call me names, shove and push me around, trip me, steal things from me, make fun of me, hit me, and other very cruel things. Fifth grade was our worst year when a teacher said that I was not allowed to play with the other kids. I made my first four friends in sixth grade.

On April 17, 2003, my mom sat me down and told me about my diagnoses of HFA and ADHD. I was a little shocked at first and then angry and embarrassed. But after a while I thought about it and realized that I had a name for my problems and was relieved about it. I only told my four friends.

Soon, seventh grade came and I was *determined* to make lots of true friends and somehow "cure" myself. I did make friends but, as before, some of them only wanted to take advantage of me. Rumors started about me. Some of them are so ridiculous that, to this day, I still laugh about them. Others are so cruel and unusual that I have to force it from my mind before I get depressed. That year I started having depressive and panic attacks. My stress and anxiety level went up.

Eighth grade, age 14 was, by far, the worst year of my life. People who I thought were my friends were making fun of me and starting rumors about me. I stopped hanging out with my true friends and went to be by myself. I refused to talk to anybody, teachers included. I would slap, bite, and pinch myself. I even tried cutting once but the sight and smell of blood was too much for me. I thought about suicide a lot.

One day, in January 2005, I refused to go to school. I was crying hysterically and said if they *did* send me to school that I would commit suicide. The next week I started home schooling, and soon I started seeing a psychologist and taking medication. I slowly started to get better. But I still had depressive and panic attacks. I still had flashbacks. I wanted to make friends so badly but didn't know how. So I bought lots of books on how to make friends and read books about autism that my mom bought to better understand myself.

In January 2006, I went to a social skills group for kids my age with the same problems. I was excited. I needed the basics in social skills and was also hoping to make friends who were like me. After I got there, I noticed a girl sitting at a table by herself. In went over and introduced myself. Her name is Elizabeth, she has Asperger Syndrome, and we have been best friends ever since.

After social skills group therapy, I joined a lot of groups and made lots of new friends with my social skills. I was happier than ever.

I would say that the past two months have been the happiest I have ever been. I have lots of great friends and I have a lot of talents and hobbies. I have hopes and dreams. And I am no longer scared to tell people that I have a mild case of autism. In fact, some of them don't believe me. Only professionals and those who are on the autism spectrum themselves know that I have HFA, but they think that I have a very mild case of Asperger Syndrome.

Oh, and I am learning to forgive my tormentors. Sometimes, I allow myself to remember and let myself cry. Other times, I grin to myself and say, "You laugh at me because I'm different ... I laugh at you because you are all the same!"

Life Excerpts

By Elizabeth, at age 17

Life with AS is quite the adventure. It's one of those "trial and error" things. If you get to the school cafeteria and realize it's too noisy to do anything, you learn not to go back during lunch. Small accommodations have made the difference in my mainstreaming success. I guess you get the best feeling of how my life is by reading through a day (or week, or however much you like) of my journal. The thing I stress to everyone is how important communication is.

Communication happens a variety of ways with me. I sign pretty well. I've taught my friends a bit. I also fingerspell. I write. Sometimes I talk. Other times I act. Other times, my friends seem to read my mind. I'm not always a good communicator in person. In fact, I'm told a lot that only gibberish comes out of my mouth when I'm excited. Which is why I like journaling online. My friends can read what I was really thinking/trying to say and we can continue it there or pick it up in person the next day.

I'm lucky to have wonderful relationships with a ton of friends who care about me as just another teenager (instead of treating me like I have mental retardation and am a giddy person 24/7 ... which some people will actually do). A lot of the relationships have blossomed through youth church choir. I'm in huge varieties in my relationships with teachers. Some teachers I hug, some I've never spoken a word to. I love most of the people in my life, and care a lot about them. But I've never had "crush" – I guess that's just a feeling I will never have. I pretty much see guys and girls as equal friends.

The following are excerpts from Elizabeth's online journal.

7/16/04
128·128
137(^2)73
What is the magic sum of a 19x19 magic square?
14(14)
11x53
[2^20(4^10)]/8^5

You should be able to do each of these problems easily. The only one I wouldn't expect you to do in your head is the magic square one. Have fun. Now the questions I can't answer I'll go get from Jacob-for my SLP hw. How am I supposed to learn to tell what the difference is between a tired face and a sad face and a frustrated face? Then there's happy vs confused vs anxious vs (on and on). Don't take that ability for granted. I work and study a ton and am no better at it than a preschooler (literally). Now with math, you study and you get better ... and you can be taught how to do all the above problems easily.

I've done my service. Gift Shop had me answer the phone, their mistake. A poor long distance caller had to deal with me.

2-11-05
Today, *they* (I'm not really sure who I'm referring to) threw everything in the book at me, short only of the fire alarm (and the trumpet rendition of Rocky in the pep assembly surely makes up for that). And I passed the test with flying colors! (Look at this metaphorical language ... the idioms!)

yep, talked to [name deleted] today. She honestly doesn't listen to a thing I say. She hears that I'm talking (or mumbling/rambling) & has no clue what. she just doesn't listen. she asked "how are you? I'll bet you're fine." to which I replied "romeo, o romeo, wherefore art thou romeo?" and she just goes on "are you going to Lunch or CA?" (I repeat my quote of shakespeare) and she goes "well have fun! I'll see you next week. bye!" *ROLLS EYES* would it kill her to treat me like a teenager instead of a preschooler? but ya know, whatever suits her.

2-23-05
and I definitely did the lunch line by myself today.

9/2/05
almost had a fire. things are alright now. we hope. and the kids are driving me crazy. piano lessons were torture with the electrical problem and I've literally locked them out of the house. they keep ringing the doorbell and pounding on the windows. Rrrrrrrr One just purposefully scraped a knee so I would have to unlock it and get them first aid. It never ends. and now Matthew is explaining theoretically how one would get up on our roof to go down the chimney. *gives up*

This weekend I'm hoping/counting-on that maybe some of you will help with various excuses in getting me out of the house. Please. So the Millers aren't even here and I'm this close ... to overload. This just stinks. But. Seeings as I can't get any hw done or anything productive, I'll just have to sit. and wait. and go crazy.

9/6/05
it [dr appt] went so well! I've never ever done so well. I was so happy and proud. besides the point. they kicked dad out.

I guess at 16 he's not allowed to stay with me? fine, fine. as always the dr asked me if I had anything to tell her or questions. of course. she had fun. she genuinely cares but she just doesn't get it. thought I was in a bunch of SPED classes. *shrug* doctors ... but today went so well I wasn't even screwed up schedule-wise and was able to return to school and continue learning.

9/9/05
2nd hour Latin was supposed to be the SLP coming to get me. After a bit I went to look for her, the poor new person. So I scared off 1 this year already. Apparently she was sitting in the special ed office. She knew she was supposed to get me but couldn't read the high school schedule and find her way around. So she hoped I'd come to her. Niiiiice. Apparently it's her first time in a high school. think about that. so speech pretty much sucked. All she cares is that I start communicating VERBALLY. I dunno if she's genuinely caring or not. *shrug* I'm back to the middle school thing of "conversation tracking." some people are *so* clueless.

out to dinner ... saw this man waving at me. I saluted and then thought hard without help. then I noticed the woman next to him: Joyce! then next to her: Sara! I guess that man was Mr B. That was pretty awesome seeing them there. Even if the restaurant was noisy and a long wait.

10-19-05
to lunch. or so I thought. PA SYSTEM: "Due to a medical emergency, bells will not ring on time. Please keep students in the classrooms." or something like that. a janitor saw me and told me to get in the nearest classroom. so I ran down to the 400s and joined LaTerza's class. I think that's her name ... but

yeah, upperclassmen are rowdy. and of course it just screws my day up completely. cause I don't get released 5 mins early now. then later the bells rang.

and I had to go with all that insanity. I went right to choir. no lunch for me today. hung out trying to cool down in there. by the end I was cooled back down. (block day helped). I was also hungry. I kind of played piano w/ Jackie AND Erin. I was pretty out of it there for a while. I know I didn't recognize ANYONE who stopped me in the music hallway. but I remember teaching Canon LH melody to someone. so choir class rowdiness is not cool.

12-4-05 [contemplating going on tour with church choir] ... makes me wonder what people do/don't know about me. Does Robert know about my lack of independent living skills? furthermore, does Joyce? (obviously she got a small taste at retreat ... ya know, with me getting zero hours of sleep). if so, how'd they find out? if not, how could they *not* figure out something's up? yeah, being me sometimes sucks in that way. ya can't send me off for an extended period of time like tour and not have a lot of explaining to do. but still, all the music and learning sound like fun to me. I would really like to do it if I had somebody I knew could keep me on the right track.

12-14-05
the vast majority of people overlook how important [communication] really is. they don't understand how lucky they are to communicate with such ease. communication has the potential to bring on all emotions. it's a way of connecting with others, of sharing and learning. and it's really funny sometimes.

lunch. [Name deleted] drives me insane. INSANE, you hear me? Someone I see daily. It wouldn't kill her to treat me like a competent, thinking high-schooler, would it? Instead of a two-year-old who needs to be spoken to loudly and slowly. *shrug* year two. you can't win sometimes.

12-16-05
something hit me today. figuratively. the drama people. They are the ones I need to be practicing my (soon-to-be fabulous) conversation skills. they are very amazing. and they're very good talkers. and they all are very good at keeping a conversation going when someone messes up. why'd it take me so long to figure that one out?

2-6-06
ajdflksj;aiweljf;lwaekj;

that, my friends, is in honor of the gibberish that came out of my mouth whenever I tried to speak today. 90% of what came out of my mouth was not in any real language. I'm not even kidding.

4-4-06
sensory overload. brought to you courtesy of the choir concert.

4-5-06
struggles ... within my mind ... regarding humanity

what I heard/saw Sunday. the video today in AP Euro. walking home humming In Remembrance and being startled out of deep thought by a neighbor driving by, waving at me. and me just thinking, hoping she lives long enough so her kids will have wonderful memories before the cancer takes the life from her.

people have enough problems with the world. so why do they make things harder by turning against each other?

INNOCENT...what does it *really* mean? (intended as rhetorical ... just think about it ... or answer if you wish)

By Erich

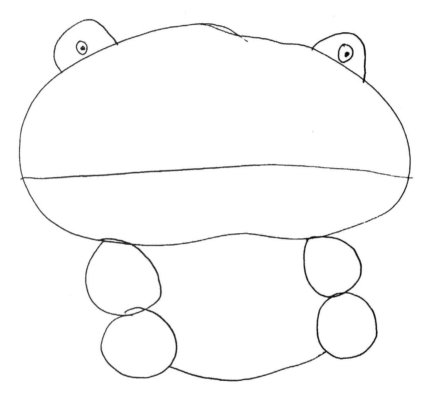

By Rilind

Just Sweet Kids

"I am thankful for laughter, except when milk comes out my nose."

–Woody Allen

When we spend so much time looking at what makes children with Asperger's special and different, we have to be careful not to lose perspective. Because you know what? Ultimately, they're really not little professors or future computer geeks. They're just sweet kids who want to be loved and accepted, just like everyone else.

By Erich

I Wish

By Otto, at age 8

I wish …
- Pokémon were real
- Every day was Saturday
- Poor people were rich
- Everyone who saw me was my friend
- For people to play video games and not get dumb
- For me to do anything I want to

My Wishes

By Eric, at age 9

I wish that everyone was nice.
I wish that everyone could feel what I feel.
I wish I could teleport.
I wish that I could turn into any Pokémon.
I wish I had $100,000,000,000.

One-of-a-Kind

Forrest, at age 3

"I wish my eyes were yellow because
that's my favorite color."

Popsicley

Andrew, at age 6

*One day Andrew and his mother were eating an afternoon snack.
He'd already had a dish of ice cream and a box of crackers.*

Andrew: "I'm so hungry. Can I have a popsicle?"

Mom: "No. That's enough to eat until dinner. Why don't
you get some lemonade?"

Andrew: "I'm not thirsty. I'm popsicley!"

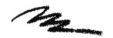

Homework

By Evelyn, at age 8

Homework is an ugly shark
that gulps up fun
making itself boring.

My Wonderful Winter Friend

By Max, at age 8

One snowflake at a time grows into one snowball. One huge snowball topped with one smaller snowball and then topped with one baby snowball turns into a wonderful winter friend. When I see him every morning he says, "Hello" with a whisper. We have a snowball fight, but he just grows bigger, one snowball at a time. He loves his fresh carrot nose each day. Unfortunately, the bunnies are stealing his nose one night at a time. He doesn't mind sharing his nose with his furry friends. I think the snow bunnies are enjoying their carrot cake for dessert each night. My fantastic snow friend visits each winter. He makes winter my favorite season. When he is not here he is in the Arctic making new friends.

Dear Santa

By Khalid, at age 8

Dear Santa,

How are you? If you ask, I'm fine. How is Mrs. Claus? Are your reindeer okay? Do you know the tooth fairy? If so, please ask her to give me two 50 cent pieces. Here's a map. Please follow instructions.

Love Khalid

My Braces

By Bridget, at age 9

I got my braces on January 2nd. I kind of like having braces even though I have problems eating. My friends think their cute and so do my parents and my sister. They are silver with pink rubber bands. I have gotten better at chewing over the next few days. They still kind of hurt, but in a few more days it will probably get better. By the way, Brenda likes them too. And Suzanne and Don like them too. And I know that everybody likes them because they said nice things about them.

School

By Bridget, at age 9

I like going to school. I like P.E. and library and recess. I like P.E. because I like to do sports. I like library because I like to check out books. I think Mrs. Taylor just ordered some new books this school year, for the kindergarteners and first graders. I like recess because I like to play and have fun. Mrs. Reynolds added five new pieces of equipment to the playground this year, and she even painted the walls green and yellow. Sometimes Don takes me, and sometimes mom takes me. So far, Suzanne picks me up every day. When will mom pick me up?

The Littlest Philanthropist

Forrest, at age 4

One of the neighbors surprised Forrest's brother with a birthday card and $10 enclosed. Forrest's brother was very excited and told Mom he wanted to use it for a Game Boy.

Forrest: "No! Use it for cancer research!"

Prayer

Forrest, at age 5

Forrest heard the siren of a passing ambulance.

Forrest: "Did you pray?"

Mom: "What?"

Forrest: "Dear God, please make sure whoever's in the ambulance feels better soon."

I Have a Dream

By Max, at age 9

I have a dream to stop animal cruelty. Too many people have been arrested because of animal cruelty and they should not have been if they were kind and loving to animals. If kids are educated about animals at an early age, they would understand animals better and know that animals have feelings and emotions too. Animal cruelty has no place in an educated mind. This is one way we can stop cruelty to animals.

What's Wrong with the World?

By Zak, at age 10

What's wrong with the world?

With wars strangling people, pollution tearing at the
Nature, racism in countries,
Hatred and fury messing our
Words …

WHAT'S WRONG WITH THE WORLD?!

Hammer Time

Forrest, at age 3

One day when Forrest was not being very nice, Dad took his toy hammer (his prized possession) away.

Forrest: "Next time take my saw. I don't like it as much."

By Joey

Index

A

Abigail, 52, 93, 158-159
Adam A, 68
Adam G, 37
Adam M, 43
Aidan, 145
Allura, 13, 44, 65, 76
Alex, 69
Andrew, 21, 25, 98, 134, 162, 196
Andrew K, 39, 61, 63
Andrew S, 85
Anna G, 94-95, 107, 119, 153-155
Avery, 47, 89

B

Breanna, 17, 19, 65, 132
Brennan, 62, 166
Bridget, 96, 198, 199

C

Casey, 181-183
Chase, 72-73
Christopher, 88
Claire, 38, 56-57, 144
Colin, 14, 114-117, 146-147, 171
Connor, 41, 99

D

Daniel, 17
Danielle, 173-174
David, 19, 20, 26, 32, 40, 74, 78, 86, 97, 108-110, 111-112, 133, 135, 142, 150-151, 156, 160, 167, 170-171
Duncan, 18, 67, 84
Dylan, 25, 101-103

E

Elizabeth, 34-35, 184-190
Eric, 195
Erich, 191, 194
Erin, 55
Evelyn, 32, 84, 197

F

Forrest, 18, 20, 22, 23, 27, 43, 61, 64, 71, 76, 79, 89, 95, 96, 131, 139, 144, 196, 199, 200, 201

G

Grace, 133
Graham, 68